Learn to Diagram with Visio® 2000

Ralph Grabowski

Wordware Publishing, Inc.

Library of Congress Cataloging-in-Publication Data

Grabowski, Ralph.
   Learn to diagram with Visio 2000 / by Ralph Grabowski.
     p. cm.
   ISBN 1-55622-709-4 (pb)
    I. Title.

   T385.G69265   2000
   650'.0285'66869--dc21   00-061456
                                              CIP

© 2001, Wordware Publishing, Inc.

All Rights Reserved

2320 Los Rios Boulevard
Plano, Texas 75074

No part of this book may be reproduced in any form or by
any means without permission in writing from
Wordware Publishing, Inc.

Printed in the United States of America

ISBN 1-55622-709-4
10 9 8 7 6 5 4 3 2
0009

Diagrams in Chapters 5, 6, and 10 used with permission of Herbert Grabowski.
Visio is a registered trademark of Microsoft Corporation.
Other product names mentioned are used for identification purposes only and may be trademarks of their respective
companies.

All inquiries for volume purchases of this book should be addressed to Wordware Publishing, Inc., at the
above address. Telephone inquiries may be made by calling:

(972) 423-0090

Contents

Contents

Acknowledgments

For the first time, a family member is involved in one of my books. My dad, Herbert Grabowski, put his 40 years of drafting and design experience into checking the lessons in this book, as well as contributing some of his hand-drafted diagrams as projects. Thanks to my wife, Heather, for her encouragement and to my children, Stefan, Heidi, and Katrina, for their enthusiasm for Dad's work.

Outside of my family, a big thank you to Judy Lemke for performing the technical editing and catching those small errors that elude the author's eye. I want to thank Jim Hill of Wordware Publishing for conceiving this book project. And thanks to Him who makes all things possible.

Introduction

Welcome to *Learn to Diagram with Visio 2000*!

This book teaches you how to diagram with Visio 2000 through ten lessons. Each lesson tackles a different kind of diagram—the kinds of diagrams that Visio is excellent at creating. These include informal maps, calendars, business forms, a variety of charts, network diagrams, and floor plans.

As you work through each lesson, you learn about Visio's tools that make it easier to create diagrams more quickly and neatly than with any other software. You can walk through the chapters of the book in order or you can jump around. Each lesson is quite independent of the others. If you are unfamiliar with Visio, then I recommend you start with Lessons 1 through 3, since they contain basic information on starting and using Visio.

About This Book

Each lesson in this book contains a wealth of learning tools:

- **What is?** Explains the purpose of the chart or diagram taught in the lesson.
- **Tutorials** Basic and advanced tutorials take you step by step through the process for creating the diagram. Each tutorial is liberally sprinkled with illustrations, so that you won't lose your way.
- **Visio resources** Describes all available resources for that particular diagram, including templates, stencils, commands, menus, and wizards.
- **Quiz** Ten questions at the end of each lesson test your knowledge. Answers are provided at the back of the book.
- **Exercises** Each lesson concludes with five diagramming problems that let you put your newfound skills to work.
- **Companion CD-ROM** The resulting diagram of all 18 tutorials is found on the CD-ROM included with this book, as well as files used in the exercises.

In addition, this book is peppered with dozens of tips that help you make the most of Visio. As a bonus, Lesson 10 contains detailed information on importing and exporting CAD drawings—information that you won't find even in Visio's documentation.

Who This Book is For

This is a task-oriented book!

Use this book in a classroom or to teach yourself Visio. Need to create a flowchart? Dive right into Lesson 5, "Create a Flowchart." Have to import an AutoCAD drawing? Check out Lesson 10, "Isometric and CAD Drawings." Want to work with data stored in an Excel spreadsheet? Look into Lesson 7, "Create a Gantt Chart."

Learn to Diagram with Visio 2000 is for anyone who needs to create charts and diagrams, but doesn't want to spend the time going through command-oriented books.

This book can be used for all editions of Visio 2000, since it was written with Visio 2000 Standard Edition in mind. Lesson 10 contains some information (DWG export) specific to Visio 2000 Technical Edition. I have made a note in the text when Technical, Professional, or Enterprise Edition has more capability than Standard Edition.

Lesson Plans

This book is divided into ten lessons. Each lesson is independent of the others; you can skip around, just like a cookbook. Every lesson (except Lesson 1) contains a basic tutorial and an advanced tutorial. I recommend that you tackle the basic tutorial. Later, when you have greater confidence in your Visio abilities, come back and try the advanced tutorials. The diagram that results from each tutorial is included on the companion CD-ROM.

You can test yourself at the end of each chapter with the ten-question quiz. Answers are provided in Appendix C. To help you put your new skills to work, each chapter concludes with five exercises. Working through the exercises helps ensure that you retain your knowledge of Visio and its commands.

Lesson 1: The Visio 2000 Tour. You tour Visio and its user interface. You learn how to start Visio several different ways, open and save files, and find your way around Visio itself. You also learn the all-important topic of reversing your errors.

Lesson 2: Create a Map. In this lesson, you learn to start Visio and open a new drawing by selecting a drawing type. The basics of dragging masters from a stencil onto a page are taught, as is Visio's Build Region command to quickly arrange map shapes on a page. You also learn how to save, print, and close the diagram.

Lesson 3: Create a Calendar. While creating a calendar, you learn how to place shapes in a diagram, use the Custom Properties dialog box to change a shape, and drag handles to change the size of a shape. You also learn how to place text in the diagram. This lesson introduces multi-page diagrams, and you learn to work with page tabs.

Lesson 4: Create Business Forms. This lesson shows you how to create business forms, including business cards and an invoice. In doing so, you learn how to use guidelines to align shapes accurately and how to edit text. In addition, you learn a variety of useful tools, such as holding down the Ctrl key to make copies of shapes, using the F4 key to repeat the last command, displaying the page margins, double-clicking text for editing, making groups of shapes, and applying backgrounds.

Lesson 5: Create a Flowchart. In this lesson, you learn about the many types of flowcharts that Visio creates. You learn how to create a basic flowchart with shapes that connect and number automatically. Then, for a change, you learn how to connect shapes manually, and how to edit connections. To help out, you learn about the Pan & Zoom window, applying a color scheme to the diagram, centering the diagram on the page, adding hyperlinks to the diagram, and finally how to bring the diagram into PowerPoint.

Lesson 6: Create an Organization Chart. You find out that there are two ways to create an organization chart in Visio: by dragging shapes onto the page or from data stored in a file. You learn to edit the chart's contents, including quickly changing the look of the chart, create a multi-page org chart, view and edit custom properties, and compare the differences between two similar org charts.

Lesson 7: Create a Gantt Chart. In this lesson, you learn how to create a Gantt chart by entering data within Visio then create a second chart by entering data external to Visio, and import it into Visio. You also learn to edit the chart and export the chart data to other applications.

Lesson 8: Create a Network Diagram. As you create a network diagram, you learn how to add custom properties to shapes, collect data, and create a report within Visio. You also learn how to export the data to an external file.

Lesson 9: Create an Office Layout. Here you learn to create a floor plan with walls, doors, windows, and furniture. You find out the importance of scale and the elements of a dimension. You learn how to add Internet hyperlinks to the furniture, export the floor plan as a Web page, then view the Web page in GIF and VML formats.

Lesson 10: Isometric and CAD Drawings. In this lesson, you learn how to display a CAD drawing in a Visio diagram, as well as to convert CAD objects into shapes. You also learn to create an isometric grid and draw isometric cubes and circles.

About the Author

Ralph Grabowski is the author of fifty books about CAD and graphics. He has authored the popular *Learn Visio* and *Learn AutoCAD* series for Wordware Publishing. This is his sixth book about Visio.

Ralph currently edits five publications: *Visions.eZine* e-newsletter for Visio and IntelliCAD users; *upFront.eZine* e-newsletter for CAD users; *CRCeZine* e-newsletter for AutoCAD users; *Design-Drawing.Com* webzine for Actrix, iGrafx, SmartSketch, and Visio users; and *AutoCAD User* magazine for AutoCAD users.

He began his work in the CAD and graphics field in 1985 as the technical editor of *CADalyst* magazine. He received his B.A.SC. degree in civil engineering from the University of British Columbia.

You can contact Ralph via e-mail at ralphg@xyzpress.com and visit his Web site at www.upfrontezine.com.

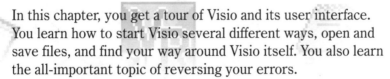

The Visio 2000 Tour

**In this
chapter, you
learn about:**

♦ **Starting Visio**

♦ **Opening files**

♦ **Saving files**

♦ **Finding your
way around
Visio**

♦ **Undo**

♦ **Stencils**

♦ **Masters**

Welcome to Visio 2000!

In this chapter, you get a tour of Visio and its user interface. You learn how to start Visio several different ways, open and save files, and find your way around Visio itself. You also learn the all-important topic of reversing your errors.

If you are an intermediate or advanced computer user, you may want to skim over the middle part of this chapter, which discusses topics unique to Visio, such as stencils and masters.

Whether a beginner or an advanced computer user, you will find that some parts of Visio are very similar to other Windows software, but some parts are very different.

Starting Visio

You can start Visio in several different ways:

From the Start Menu

Step 1. On the taskbar, click **Start**. Notice the Start menu.

Step 2. From the Start menu, select **Programs**, then select **Visio 2000**. Notice that Visio 2000 starts.

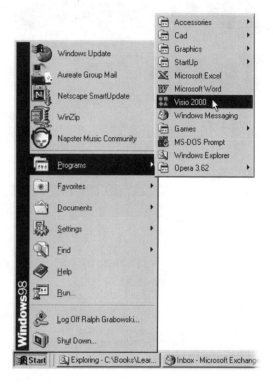

From the Windows Desktop

Step 1. Double-click the **Visio 2000** icon on the Windows desktop. If you have difficulty double-clicking the mouse's button, you can select the icon, then press the **Enter** key on the keyboard. Notice that Visio 2000 starts.

TIP: Creating a desktop icon   If you do not see the Visio 2000 icon on the desktop, users of Windows 98, ME, and 2000 can easily add one. From the Start menu, select **Programs**, then drag the Visio 2000 item onto the desktop. Notice that Windows creates a shortcut icon for Visio.

From Windows Explorer

Step 1.   In the Windows Explorer, go to a folder holding a Visio diagram. Visio diagram files have a filename extension of .vsd.

Step 2.   Double-click the icon in front of the Visio diagram filename. As an alternative, you can right-click the file, and select **Open** from the shortcut menu. Notice that Visio starts, and opens the diagram file automatically.

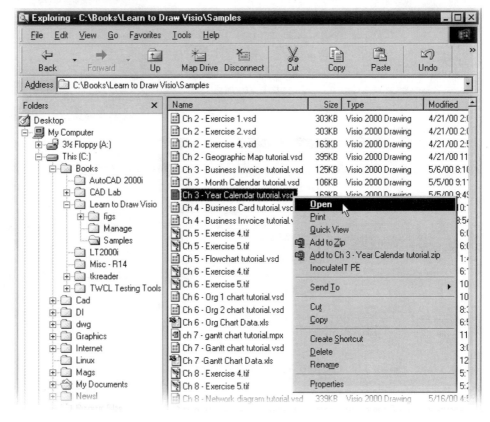

Starting with a Blank Drawing

You can start Visio with a blank drawing, but this is not the way that Visio is designed to be used. (Visio is meant to help you with solutions, which provide shapes and specific commands to help you create diagrams quickly.) Still, there may be times when you want to start Visio "from scratch." Here's how:

Step 1. Start Visio. Notice the Welcome to Visio 2000 dialog box.

Step 2. Click **Cancel**.

Step 3. From the toolbar, click the **New Drawing** button. As an alternative, you can select **File | New | New Drawing** from the menu bar. To do this more quickly, press **Ctrl+N** (hold down the **Ctrl** key and press **N** on the keyboard).

Toolbar

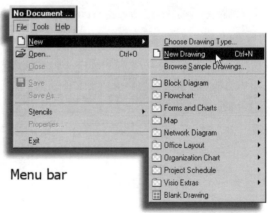

Menu bar

Notice that Visio opens a blank drawing.

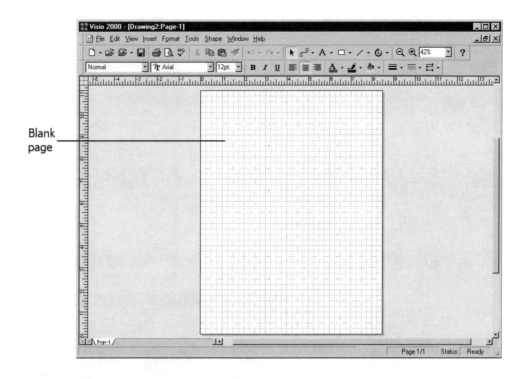

Blank
page

Starting with a Solution

The most common way to start a new diagram is to start Visio with a solution. A *solution* is Visio's term for a collection of template and stencil files, along with specialized tools and wizards. (Solutions are stored in the \Visio 2000\Solutions folder.) For example, the Office Layout solution includes:

- **Office Layout Shapes stencil**—holds the shapes for drawing office layouts.

- **Office Layout template**—specifies the scale and orientation of the page.

- **Architecture menu item**—adds several commands to the menu bar and shortcut menu.

Step 1. Start Visio. Notice the Welcome to Visio 2000 dialog box.

Step 2. In the Create new drawing area, select **Choose drawing type**.

Step 3. Click **OK**. Notice the Choose Drawing Type dialog box.

Step 4. In the Category list, choose a general category of solutions.

Step 5. In the Drawing type list, choose a specific type of solution.

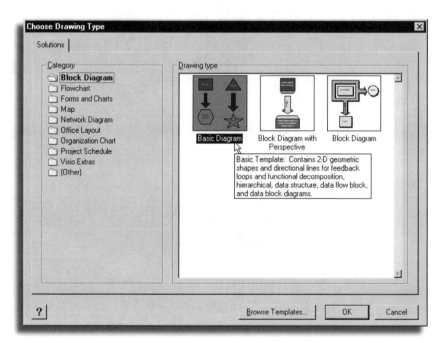

Step 6. Click **OK**. Notice that Visio opens with a blank drawing.

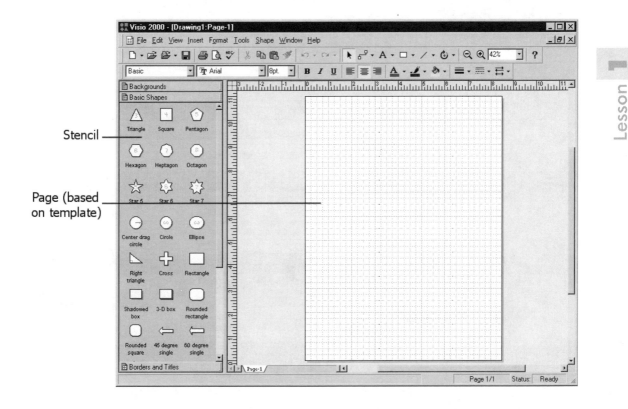

Stencil —

Page (based on template)

TIP: A second new diagram   To start another new diagram based on the same solution, simply press **Ctrl+N**. Notice that Visio displays a new blank drawing with the same stencils as before. To switch back to the previous diagram, select its name from the Window menu.

Starting with an Existing Diagram

When you want to open a diagram that you (or someone else) have worked on, follow these steps:

Step 1.   Start Visio. Notice the Welcome to Visio 2000 dialog box.

Step 2.   In the Open existing file area, select **Browse existing files**.

Step 3.   Click **OK**. Notice the **Open** dialog box.

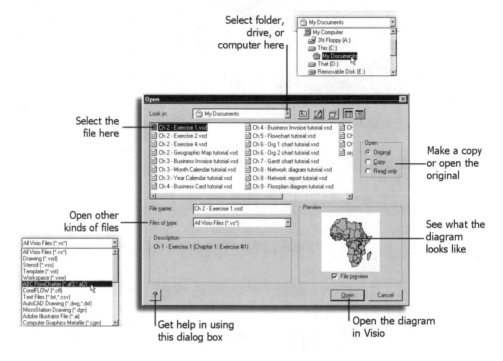

Select folder, drive, or computer here

Select the file here

Open other kinds of files

Get help in using this dialog box

Make a copy or open the original

See what the diagram looks like

Open the diagram in Visio

Step 4.   Visio normally opens this dialog box at the My Documents folder. If you store your diagrams in another folder, drive, or computer, click the **Look in** list.

TIP: Changing the default folder

If you store your diagrams in a folder other than My Documents, you can tell Visio to open there. From Visio's menu bar, select **Tools | Options**. When the Options dialog box appears, click the **File Paths** tab. In the Drawings field, enter the name of the path to the folder, such as C:\Drawings. (Notice that you can change the path for other files Visio accesses.) Click **OK** to close the dialog box.

The Open dialog box provides you with several options. You can:

- Open a copy of the diagram, instead of the original.
- Open the diagram as read-only, which means you cannot save changes you make.
- Open other kinds of files, such as those created by ABC Flowcharter and AutoCAD.

Step 5.   When you have selected the diagram to open, click **OK**. Notice that Visio opens and displays the diagram.

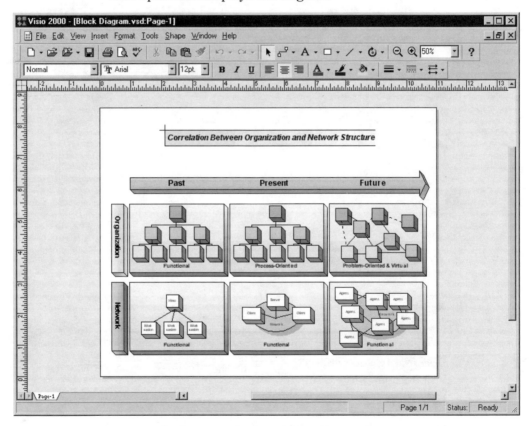

TIP: Opening sample diagrams   To open the sample diagrams that come with Visio, select **File | New | Browse Sample Drawings** from the menu bar. Visio opens the Browse Sample Drawings dialog box opened at the Sample folder.

Visio's User Interface

As a Windows user, parts of Visio should look very familiar to you—the menu bar, the toolbars, and the window controls. Other parts may be unfamiliar, such as the stencil and the pasteboard. Let's take a look at how all these work. Starting at the top of the illustration, and working our way around counter-clockwise:

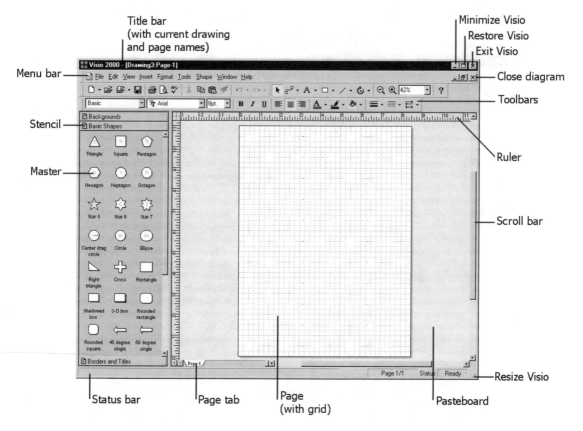

Title Bar

The title bar holds the name of the application (Visio, in this case), the current drawing, and page number. You can also use the title bar to drag the Visio window around the Windows desktop.

Menu Bar

The menu bar contains all the commands available in Visio. Commands are categorized into groups. For example, all file-related commands are listed under File.

To access a command, click the menu item, then select the command. For example, to open a diagram, select File | Open. Advanced users may be interested in customizing the menu bar.

Stencil

The stencil holds predrawn shapes. Visio includes dozens of stencils that group shapes into categories. Visio can have more than one stencil open at a time.

When the shape is still in the stencil, it is called a *master*. When the master is dragged onto the page, it becomes a *shape*. The shape in the stencil is called a master because the shape is linked back to it. If you were to change the master, the shape would change also.

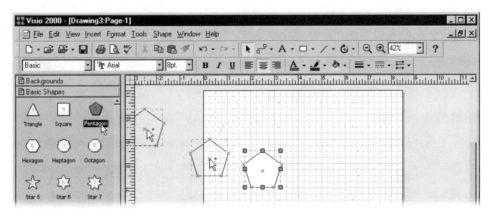

Dragging the master out of the stencil does not "use it up"; you can drag many copies of the same master onto the page. In this book, you will often read the instruction "drag the master from the stencil onto the page." We will discuss stencils in greater detail later in this chapter.

Status Bar

The status bar reports information and help text. The information typically includes the position and angle of shapes. The help text is a brief description of the selected shape or command.

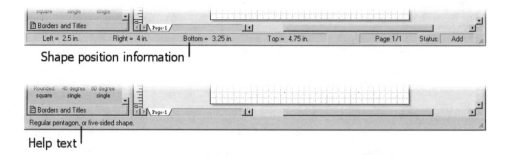

Shape position information

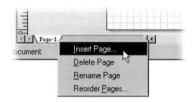

Help text

Page Tab

In many cases, a Visio diagram has a single page. You can, however, add one or more pages to the diagram to create a document. Page tabs let you move quickly between pages. Right-click the page tab to insert more pages, and reorder or delete pages.

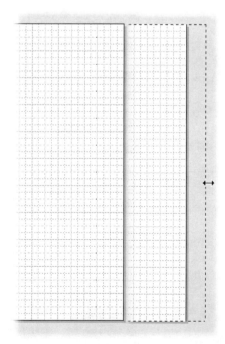

Page

The page is where the diagramming takes place. In most cases, the page represents the standard letter-size sheet of paper: 8½" x 11", also called A-size. This should match the paper in your printer unless you know how to deal with scale factors. What you see is what you get.

Via the File | Page Setup command, you can select other sizes and orientation of pages, including metric. As an alternative, you can hold down the Ctrl key and drag the edge of the page to make it larger or smaller.

The page displays a grid, which helps you align shapes. The display of the grid can be turned on and off with the View | Grid command; the gridlines are displayed and not printed. You can change the spacing of the grid lines with the dialog box displayed by Tools | Ruler & Grid.

Pasteboard

The pasteboard is the cyan (light blue) area surrounding the page. You can use this area for temporary storage of shapes, clip art, and samples of text. The pasteboard is never printed.

Resize Visio

Drag the corner of the Visio window to resize it larger and smaller. You can grab any of the four corners and the four sides to change the size of the window. It just so happens that the lower-right corner has that triangular marking.

Scroll Bar

Visio usually has three scroll bars: two in the drawing area and one in the stencil. Drag the scroll bar to see other parts of the drawing or stencil. As an alternative, you can hold down the Ctrl and Shift keys along with the right mouse button, then pan the drawing. *Pan* means to move the view.

Ruler

The drawing area has two rulers that help you measure distances in the drawing. As you move a shape on the page, small lines indicate the shape's location on the ruler. The ruler is not printed. You can turn the display of the rulers on and off: from the menu bar, select View | Rulers. The measurement units of the rulers can be changed via the Tools | Ruler & Grid command.

Toolbars

The toolbars contain buttons and list boxes that give you (usually) faster access to commands than do the menu bars.

The problem I find with toolbars is that I have to memorize the meaning of the little pictures (called *icons*) on each button. To help you out, Visio displays a piece of information. Leave the cursor over the button for a second or two, and Visio displays the *tooltip*. This small yellow rectangle explains the purpose of the button in a word or two.

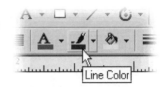

Advanced users may want to create their own toolbars or change the existing toolbars.

Close Diagram

Click the small x button and Visio closes the diagram, along with related stencils. If the diagram has not been saved, Visio asks if you want to save your valuable work.

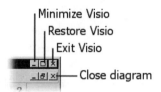

Minimize Visio
Restore Visio
Exit Visio
Close diagram

Exit Visio

The x button on the title bar closes Visio. If necessary, Visio asks if you want to save your work.

Restore Visio

The middle button with the box performs double duty:

- If Visio is running in a window, click this button to *maximize* Visio. This means that the Visio window takes up the entire desktop.

- If Visio is maximized, click this button to *restore* Visio to a smaller window.

As an alternative, you can double-click the title bar to switch between windowed and maximized.

Minimize Visio

The button with the dash *minimizes* the Visio window. This means that Visio disappears from the desktop. You bring back Visio by clicking its button on the taskbar.

Basic Mouse Moves

When you use Visio, you do a lot of selecting, dragging, and right-clicking with your mouse. Here's what these terms mean:

Selecting: Move the cursor over the shape, and press the left mouse button. Visio lets you know the shape has been selected by surrounding it with a dashed green rectangle called the *alignment box*, and eight small green-filled squares called *handles*.

- **Alignment box:** This is usually, but not always, the outer boundary of the shape. Many users don't realize that the shape is changed by its alignment box, not by the shape itself.

- **Handles:** Allow you to resize the shape, either larger, longer, shorter, or smaller.

Dragging: Dragging is used to move, copy, and resize shapes. To drag, select the shape. Continue to hold down the left mouse button while moving the mouse. When the shape is in its new location, release the mouse button.

- **Move**: Drag the shape.
- **Copy**: Hold down the Ctrl key and drag the shape. Notice that Visio displays a tiny plus sign (+) next to the cursor, which indicates that copying is taking place.
- **Resize**: Drag one of the eight handles. If a shape has tiny gray padlocks, it cannot be resized.

Right-clicking: Press the right mouse button. Right-clicking in Visio usually displays a shortcut menu, which is a menu that appears at the cursor location.

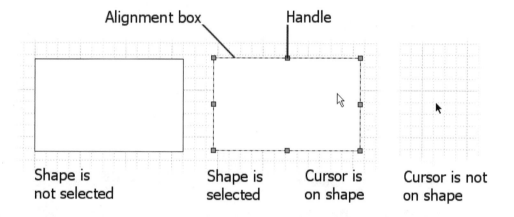

Alignment box   Handle

| Shape is not selected | Shape is selected | Cursor is on shape | Cursor is not on shape |

TIP: Cursor colors   Sometimes it can be hard to tell when the cursor is over a shape and when it isn't. Visio changes the color of the cursor to tell you the difference:

White pointer: The cursor is on a shape. If you click now, you select the shape.

Black pointer: The cursor is not on a shape. If you click now, you select the page.

There are some other mouse movements that are used less often in Visio:

Double-clicking: Pressing the left mouse button twice, quickly. Logitech mice usually have three buttons, and include software that allow you to assign the double-click to the middle button. I have found this is a great timesaver.

Roller wheel: The newest mice include a wheel between the buttons. In Visio:

- Rolling the wheel scrolls the diagram up and down.
- Holding the Shift key and rolling the wheel scrolls the diagram side to side.
- Holding the Ctrl key and rolling the wheel zooms in and out.

Keyboard: Some Visio commands function together with the keyboard. Earlier, I mentioned holding down the Ctrl key to make a copy. Another example is to zoom in on the diagram by holding down the Ctrl and Shift keys, then drag a rectangle shape. Appendix A lists all the keyboard and mouse shortcuts available in Visio.

Using Stencils

The philosophy behind Visio is to use predrawn shapes to quickly create diagrams. The shapes in Visio are based on the green plastic stencils used by manual drafters. To physically draw a shape, the drafter would run a mechanical pencil around the inside of a shape in the plastic stencil.

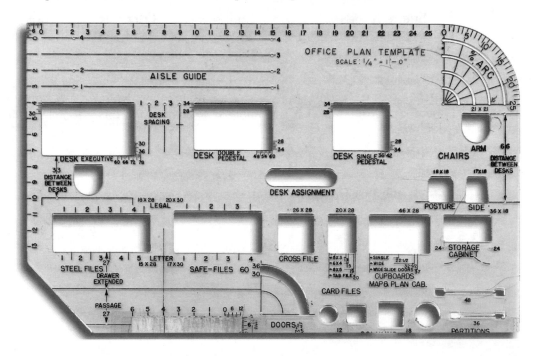

Visio shapes are collected in stencils, which even retain the green color of their heritage. To draw a shape, you drag the shape from the green "electronic" stencil onto the page. (Technically, while still in the stencil, the shape is called a master. When the master is dragged onto the page, it becomes a shape.)

When you start Visio with a solution, Visio automatically opens stencils appropriate to that solution. You can also open stencils on your own: From the menu bar, select File | Stencils. Notice the list of categories. Select one.

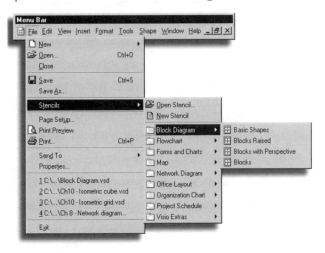

When the stencil opens, notice that most of it consists of masters, represented by icons and a couple of words of text. A menu is hidden in the icon on the stencil's title bar. A shortcut menu is available when right-clicking a master.

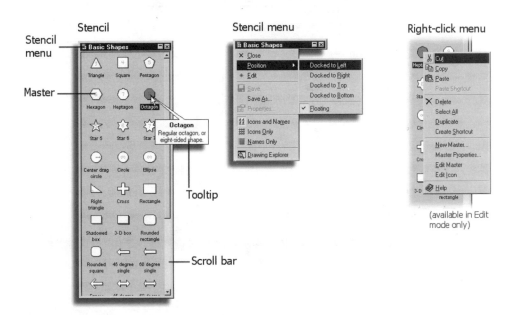

Advanced users may be interested in creating their own custom masters and stencils.

Finding Shapes with the Shape Explorer

One of the benefits of Visio is that it comes with hundreds of shapes. One of the problems with Visio is that it comes with hundreds of shapes!

Usually, I find the right shape by guessing which stencil it is in. All stencils are in the \Solutions folder. For example, I have learned that the annotation shapes are found in the Callouts.Vss stencil, which is found in the \Solutions\Visio Extras folder.

But what if I cannot remember where that special stencil is located? That's where the Shape Explorer comes in. Perhaps it would be better called the "shape finder," because that is what it does.

Select Tools | Macros | Shape Explorer from the menu bar. Notice that Visio opens the Shape Explorer.

- In the Search for field, enter as much of the wording as you can. For example, if you are looking for annotation shapes, enter "Annotation."

- Click Find Now. After a few seconds, Visio returns the result of its search. In this example, notice that it found shapes on three stencils.

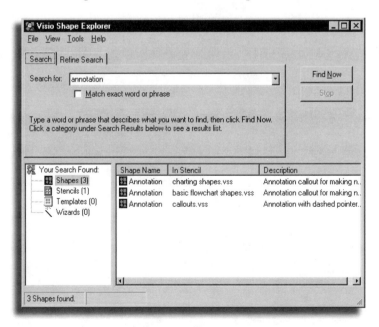

If this simple approach came back with too many results, select the Refine Search tab. This lets you narrow down the search to, say, shapes only. The Details button further refines the search.

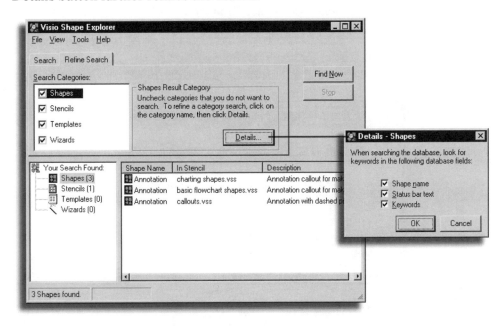

The Shape Explorer performs the find function only. A nice feature would be to be able to drag the found shape into the diagram, but this is not possible. You need to use the File | Stencil command to open the stencil in Visio.

Oops! I Made a Mistake

The best thing about making a mistake on the computer is that it can reverse your mistake, in most cases. As you work with software programs, you will find that your best friend is the Undo command.

What if you accidentally erase a whole bunch of your work from the page? From the menu bar, select Edit | Undo (or click the Undo button) and your work returns. (As an alternative, you can press Ctrl+Z.)

What if you change your mind about how you edited those shapes? Click Undo until the shape is back to the way it was.

Visio normally limits undo to the last ten steps. If your computer has a lot of memory and free disk space, you can increase this to 99 steps, as follows: From the menu bar, select Tools | Options. When the Options dialog box appears, click the General tab. Notice the Undo levels option is set to 10. Highlight the 10 and change it to 99. Click OK to dismiss the dialog box.

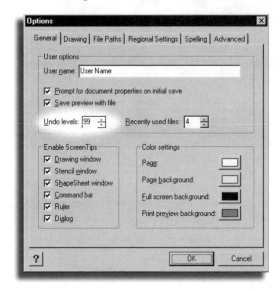

What if you change your mind about the undo? From the menu bar, select Edit | Redo (or click the Redo button) and Visio restores whatever was undone. (As an alternative, you can press Ctrl+Y.)

Indeed, power users will sometimes use Ctrl+Z and Ctrl+Y to step back and forth through a series of diagramming steps. This lets them try out different effects. Be careful, though: Undo and Redo do not work in all cases. Visio does not undo zoom and pan. If you save the diagram over an existing file, that cannot be reversed.

Saving Your Work

When it comes to saving your work, you have three strategies: (1) save the diagram over an earlier version, (2) save the diagram by a different name, or (3) save the diagram in another format.

Save

When you create a new diagram, Visio gives it the "Drawing1.vsd" name. The diagram, however, is <u>not</u> saved. To save your diagram, you can:

- Select File | Save from the menu bar.
- Press Ctrl+S.
- Click the diskette icon on the toolbar.

The first time you save the diagram, Visio displays the Save As dialog box. This gives you the opportunity to change the diagram's name to something more meaningful than "Drawing1." You enter a name of up to 255 characters long. Click Save.

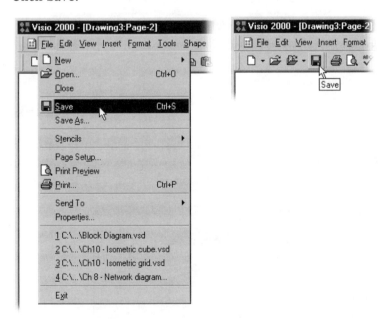

You must save each diagram individually. Visio does not have an automatic save feature, as is found in some other software programs.

Save As

To save the diagram by a different filename, choose File | Save As from the menu bar. When the Save As dialog box appears, enter a different name, or select a different folder. Click Save.

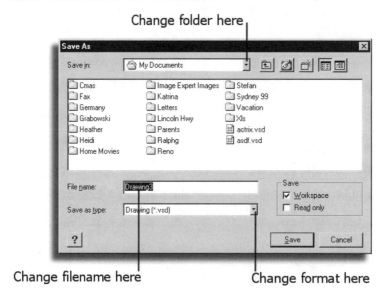

Export

To save the diagram in a different format, choose File | Save As from the menu bar. When the Save As dialog box appears, select the format from the Save as type list. Click Save. In some cases, Visio displays the Output Filter Setup dialog box, which allows you to select options.

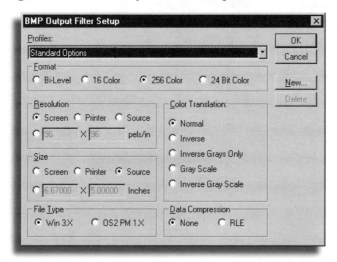

Closing Diagrams and Exiting Visio

To close the diagram, you can:

- Select File | Close from the menu bar.
- Press Ctrl+F4.
- Click the small x button below the title bar.

You do not need to close the diagram before exiting Visio. To exit Visio, you can:

- Select File | Exit from the menu bar.
- Press Alt+F4.
- Click the x button at the right end of the title bar.

In all cases, Visio asks if you want to save your work—if you have not already done so. In most cases, click Yes; click No only if you are sure that you don't want to save the changes you made to the diagram. Click Cancel to return to Visio, and continue working.

Quiz

1. You can start Visio by double-clicking a VSD (Visio drawing file) in Windows Explorer.

   True / False

2. Match the abbreviation with its meaning:

a.	Ctrl	i.	Redo.
b.	Shift	ii.	Hold down the Ctrl key.
c.	Ctrl+N	iii.	Undo.
d.	Ctrl+Z	iv.	Hold down the Shift key.
e.	Ctrl+Y	v.	Start a new drawing.

3. Visio can only open diagrams that it has created.

   True / False

4. When a shape is in the stencil, it is called a:

   a. Shape.

   b. Super shape.

   c. Master.

   d. Stencil shape.

5. A Visio drawing contains a single page.
   True / False

6. The page in a Visio drawing:

   a. Can be any size.

   b. Is limited to letter size.

   c. Is limited to sizes supported by the printer.

   d. Is limited to sizes supported by the solution.

7. The gridlines are printed along with the rest of the drawing.
   True / False

8. A tooltip:

   a. Is a Visio drawing tool.

   b. Is a Visio editing tool.

   c. Explains the meaning of life.

   d. Explains the purpose of a toolbar button.

9. The purpose of handles is:

   a. Moving the shape.

   b. Resizing the shape.

   c. Copying the shape.

   d. Erasing the shape.

10. When the pointer cursor is black, this means that:

    a. Visio is busy completing a command.

    b. The cursor is over a shape.

    c. The cursor is not over a shape.

    d. Visio has locked up.

Exercises

1. Start and exit Visio three different ways.

2. Start Visio with the Basic Diagram solution. Drag some masters from the stencil onto the page. Exit Visio with Alt+F4; do not save your work.

3. Start Visio with no solution. Open the Format Shape and View toolbars. Drag toolbars away from their docked position, so that they float. Practice returning floating toolbars to a docked position—it's tricky!

4. Continuing from exercise #2, drag several masters onto the page. Use the handles to change the size of the shapes. Move the shapes to other places on the page. Make a copy of one shape. After making the copy, press function key F4; notice what happens.

5. Continuing from exercise #4, use the Undo and Redo commands to reverse your changes.

Lesson

Create a Map

What is a Map?

Even though you probably are familiar with maps, you should know that Visio 2000 provides two kinds of maps: geographic and directional maps.

A *geographic map* shows the outline of countries, such as Yemen and Germany, along with major rivers and lakes. In addition, Visio provides outlines of states and provinces for the three North American countries—Canada, Mexico, and the United States. These map shapes are scaled relative to each other, and are more accurate in Visio 2000 than in earlier versions of Visio.

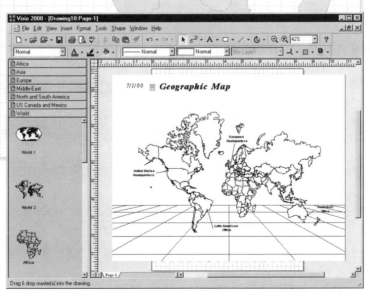

A *directional map* is meant to show you how to get somewhere; the map is symbolic rather than accurate. Visio provides many shapes for creating this kind of map.

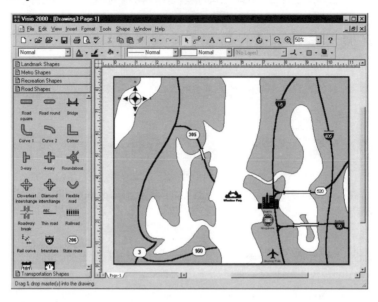

Tutorials

In the following tutorials, you create a geographic map and a directional map.

Basic: Making a Geographic Map

In this basic tutorial, you quickly create a geographic map of Europe by dragging all map shapes onto the page, then having Visio arrange the shapes.

Step 1. Start Visio 2000 by double-clicking its icon on the Windows Desktop. As an alternative, you can start Visio from the menu bar by clicking **Start | Programs | Visio 2000**. Notice the Welcome to Visio 2000 dialog box.

Step 2.   Select **Choose drawing type**, and click **OK**. Notice the Choose Drawing Type dialog box.

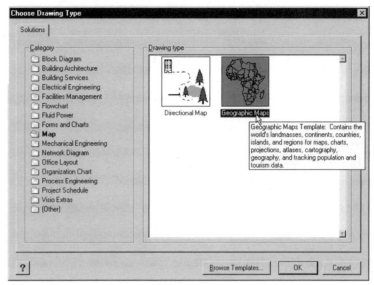

TIP: Viewing tooltips   Pause the cursor over items in the Drawing type preview window to see a tooltip (text in a yellow box that pops up near the cursor) that describes the solution.

Step 3.   Under Category, select **Map**. The number of items you see in the Category listing varies according to the edition of Visio 2000 installed on your computer. The list shown in the illustration is from Visio 2000 Technical Edition.

Step 4.   In the Drawing type preview window, select **Geographic Maps**. Click **OK**. Notice that Visio opens a blank page, along with several map stencils on the left. The stencils segregate the map masters into seven groups: Africa, Asia, Europe, Middle-East, North and South America, US Canada and Mexico, and World.

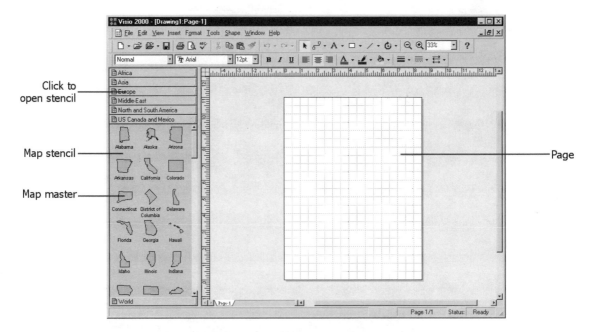

Click to
open stencil

Map stencil

Map master

Page

Step 5.   Click the **Europe** stencil's header to display the European map masters (① and ②). Drag the stencil's scroll bar down to see all the map masters ③: country borders, major lakes, and major rivers. (Some country borders may be incorrect because of changes due to politics and wars.)

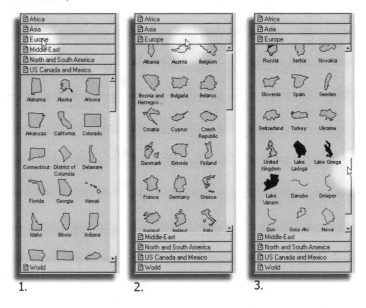

1.   2.   3.

Step 6.   Right-click the **Europe** stencil. Notice the shortcut menu.

Step 7. Select **Select All** ①.
Notice that all masters turn
blue in color ②; this is how
Visio tells you that it has
selected all masters. Pause
the cursor over a master in
the stencil to see a tooltip
that describes the master.

Step 8. With all the masters
selected, drag any one of
the masters onto the page.
Notice that the map shapes
line up in a diagonal line.
(When a master is dragged
onto a page, it becomes a
shape.)

1.

2.

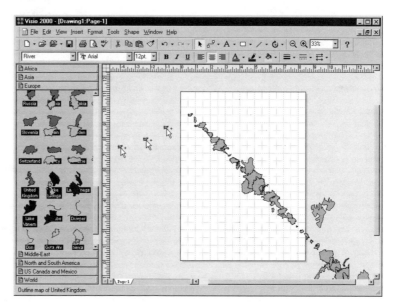

Step 9. Visio is able to put the map together automatically. Press **Ctrl+A** to
select all shapes (hold down the **Ctrl** key and press **A**).

From the menu bar, select **Tools**, then select **Build Region** ①.
Notice that Visio displays the Build Region dialog box ②; ensure that
a check mark appears next to Size shapes to fill the drawing page (if
not, click the white box to make the check mark appear). Click **OK**.

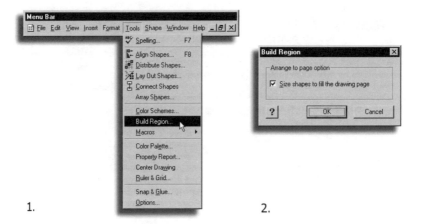

1.

2.

Notice that Visio takes a couple of seconds to arrange the shapes into a single map of Europe.

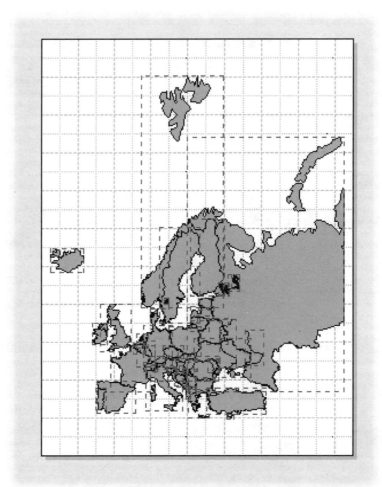

TIP: Selection rectangles The magenta selection rectangles (pink boxes) are Visio's way of showing you that it has selected all shapes on the page. To remove the selection rectangles, click anywhere on the *pasteboard* (the cyan (light blue) area surrounding the page).

This completes the tutorial for creating a geographic map. If you wish, you can use the techniques below to save and print the map.

Useful Techniques

Save the Drawing

Press **Ctrl+S**. Notice that Visio displays the Save As dialog box. Enter a name, select a folder, and click Save. Click **OK** in the Properties dialog box.

Print the Drawing

Press **Ctrl+P**. Notice the Print dialog box. If necessary, select a printer, and specify the printer's properties. When ready, click **OK**.

Close the Drawing

To close the drawing, select **File | Close** (from the menu bar, select **File**, then select **Close**).

Exit Visio

To exit Visio 2000, select **File | Exit**. As a shortcut, you can click the small x at the extreme right end of Visio's title bar.

Advanced: Making a Directional Map

In this advanced tutorial, you create a directional map of a road.

Step 1. With Visio still open from the basic tutorial, click the down arrow next to the New Drawing button on the Standard toolbar.

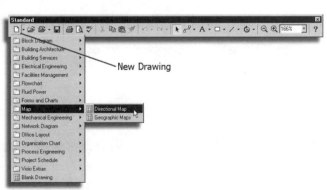

Step 2. Select **Map | Directional Map**. Notice that Visio opens a new draw-ing, along with a different set of stencils.

Step 3. Create a simple roadway map by dragging several road masters onto the page. To help create your map, follow these tips:

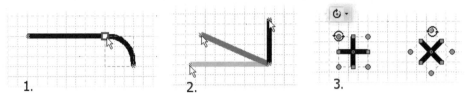

1.   2.   3.

- To select a shape, click it; Visio surrounds the shape with a green rectangle. To select two or more shapes, hold down the Shift key, then click the shapes.
- The cursor changes color from black to white when the cursor is over a shape.
- When the end of one road connects to another, a red square shows up ①.
- To rotate one-dimensional shapes, like a road, drag one end around ②.
- To rotate two-dimensional shapes, like an intersection, click the Rotation tool (on the toolbar), then drag one of the green, round handles around ③.
- When rotating a shape, you can constrain the rotation to 45-degree angles by holding down the Shift key while rotating.

Step 4. Click the **Landmark Shapes** stencil. Drag some more masters onto the page. Here are some more diagramming tips:

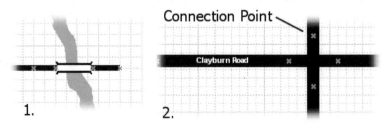

Connection Point

Clayburn Road

1.   2.

- To make one shape appear "underneath" another shape (such as water under a bridge), select the water shape and press Ctrl+B ("B" is short for back) ①. To make the shape appear "on top" of another, select the shape and press Ctrl+F ("F" is short for foreground).

- To make a copy of a shape already on the page, hold down the Ctrl key and drag the shape. Notice that Visio makes a copy of the shape.
- To add text to most shapes, double-click the shape. Type the text, then click anywhere else in the drawing ②.
- The small blue x is called a *connection point*, and it shows you where shapes connect ②.

Step 5. Save your drawing, and print it out. If you wish, you may close the drawing and exit Visio at this time.

Visio Resources

Visio 2000 provides the following resources for creating maps. The templates and stencils are found in the \Visio 2000\Solutions\Map folder.

Related Templates

Directional Map.Vst
Geographic Maps.Vst

Related Stencils

Geographic maps:

Africa.Vss
Asia.Vss
Europe.Vss
Middle-East.Vss
North and South America.Vss
US Canada and Mexico.Vss
World.Vss
Flags.Vss

Directional maps:

Landmark Shapes.Vss
Metro Shapes.Vss
Recreation Shapes.Vss
Road Shapes.Vss
Transportation Shapes.Vss

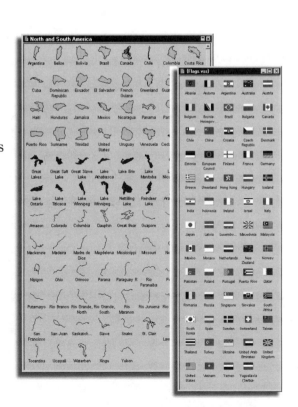

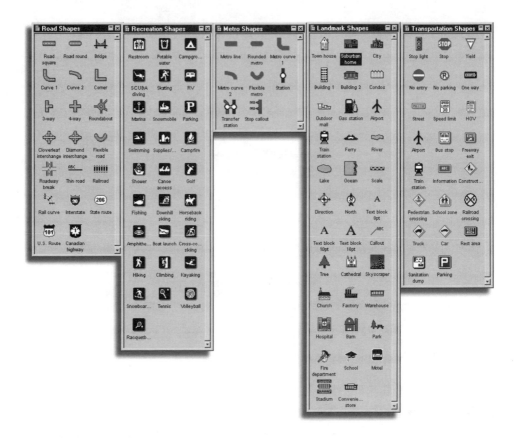

Related Commands

Tools | Build Region

The Build Region command automatically joins map shapes appropriately. For example, when you drag the British Columbia and Washington shapes onto a page, Build Region correctly joins the bottom border of British Columbia province to the top border of Washington state.

In addition, the command optionally resizes the map shapes to fit the page. The command displays a dialog box with the "Size shape to fit the drawing page" option. By default, the option is turned on.

This command is usually available only when you open the Geographic Maps template file, because it does not work for all shapes; it works only for shapes that have been "enabled for arranging." You can also find the command when you right-click an enabled shape, as well as under Tools | Macros | Maps | Build Region.

Related Toolbars

The Format Shape toolbar displays line and fill styles for modifying the look of map elements. The toolbar displays a different selection of predefined styles for geographic maps and directional maps.

Geographic maps:

Directional maps:

Summary

In this chapter, you learned how to create geographic and directional maps. In addition, you learned how to open solutions (template drawings), save your work, and print drawings.

Quiz

1. Visio's Geographic Map solution allows you to:
    a.   Create maps showing average annual rainfall.
    b.   Create maps showing country borders.
    c.   Create directional maps.
    d.   Play extended games of Risk.

2. Visio's Directional Map solution allows you to:
    a.   Create maps showing visitors how to get to your house.
    b.   Create maps showing gross national product.
    c.   Create geographic maps.
    d.   Play extended games of Monopoly.

3. To quickly join all shapes in a geographic map, use the following command:
    a.   Join Shapes.
    b.   Create World Peace.
    c.   Attach Borders.

    d.   Build Region.

4. When a shape is in a stencil, it is called a:

    a.   Master.

    b.   Shape.

    c.   Diagram.

    d.   Symbol.

5. Geographic shapes have country borders, major lakes, and rivers on separate layers.

    True / False

6. Match the shortcut keystroke with its meaning:

    a.   Ctrl+A   i.   Save file.

    b.   Ctrl+B   ii.   Move to back.

    c.   Ctrl+P   iii.   Select all.

    d.   Ctrl+S   iv.   Start a new drawing.

    e.   Ctrl+N   v.   Print drawing.

7. To rotate two-dimensional shapes, you would:

    a.   From the menu bar, select Shape | Rotate.

    b.   Click the Rotation tool, then drag a handle around.

    c.   Drag one end around.

    d.   Do nothing, since two-dimensional shapes cannot be rotated.

8. When a master is dropped on a page, it is called a:

    a.   Master.

    b.   Page element.

    c.   Shape.

    d.   Symbol.

9. To place a shape at right angles, hold down the:

    a.   Alt key.

    b.   Ctrl key.

    c.   Spacebar.

    d.   Shift key.

10. Visio can only use geographic map shapes on geographic maps.

    True / False

Exercises

1. Using the Geographic Map solution, create a map of Africa. Follow the steps described in the basic tutorial. Your completed map should be similar to the map in the adjacent illustration.

2. Once you create the map of Africa in exercise #1, turn off the Rivers and Lakes layers. (If you were unable to create the map, use the Ch 2 - Exercise 1.vsd file provided on the companion CD-ROM.)

3. Print the map you created in exercise #1.

4. Create a directional map that shows a visitor how to get to your home from the nearest major highway or freeway. An example is shown in the illustration.

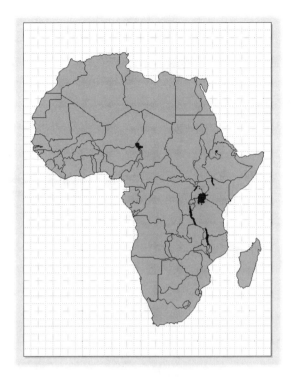

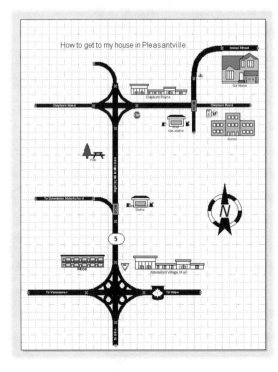

5. Use the Metro Shapes stencil to create a subway map. If your city has a subway system, try copying it. If not, follow the portion of the London Subway shown in the illustration.

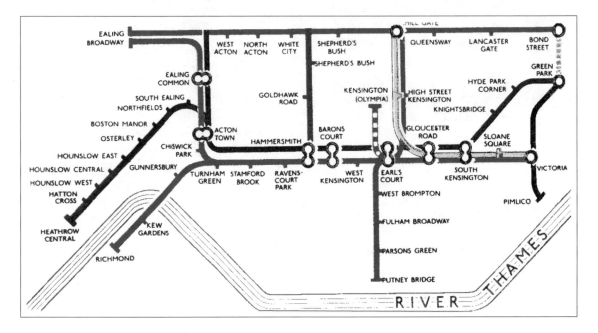

Create a Calendar

What is a Calendar?

There are many different kinds of calendars: month calendars, desk calendars that show one day at a time, wall calendars that show a quarter (three months) or entire year at a time, daytimers that show a day or week at a time, and even those found in electronic devices, like the Palm computer. Many calendars start the week with Sunday, but some start the week with Saturday or Monday.

Visio creates two kinds of calendars: month and year. The month calendar displays an entire month on a page; you can create a multi-month calendar by placing each month on a separate page. When you drag the Large month master onto the page, it displays a dialog box providing you with a number of options (see the basic tutorial for details).

In this chapter, you learn about:

- ◆ Placing shapes in a diagram

- ◆ Using the Custom Properties dialog box to change a shape

- ◆ Dragging handles to change the size of a shape

- ◆ Placing text in the diagram

- ◆ Creating a multi-page diagram

- ◆ Working with page tabs

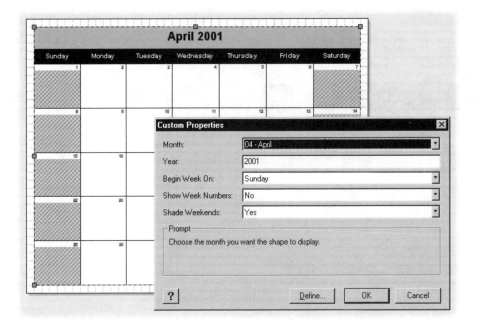

The year calendar displays the entire year on a page. When you drag the Yearly calendar master onto the page, it displays the Custom Properties dialog box with the following options:

Property	Options	Default
Year	Type a year, such as 2001.	Current year
Begin Week On	Select Sunday or Monday.	Sunday

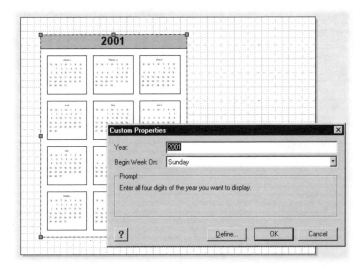

Tutorials

In the following tutorials, you create a one-month calendar, then a 12-month calendar.

Basic: Making a One-month Calendar

In this basic tutorial, you quickly create a one-month calendar useful for, say, planning your vacation trip, then populate it with useful shapes.

Step 1.   Start Visio 2000 by double-clicking its icon on the Windows Desktop. As an alternative, you can start Visio from the menu bar by clicking **Start | Programs | Visio 2000**. Notice the Welcome to Visio 2000 dialog box.

Step 2.   Double-click **Choose drawing type**. Notice the Choose Drawing Type dialog box.

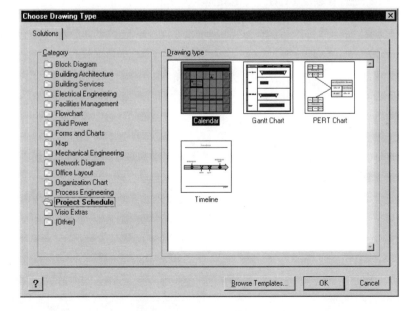

Step 3. Under Category, select **Project Schedule**.

Step 4. In the Drawing type preview window, double-click **Calendar.** Click **OK**. Notice that Visio opens a blank page, along with a calendar stencil on the left.

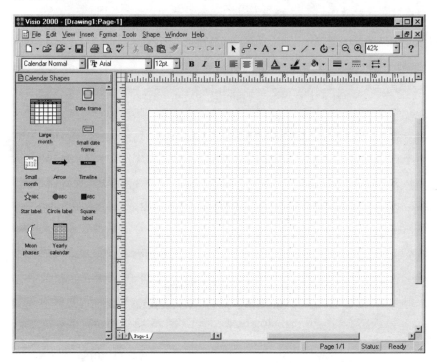

Step 5. From the Calendar Shapes stencil, drag the **Large month** master onto the page.

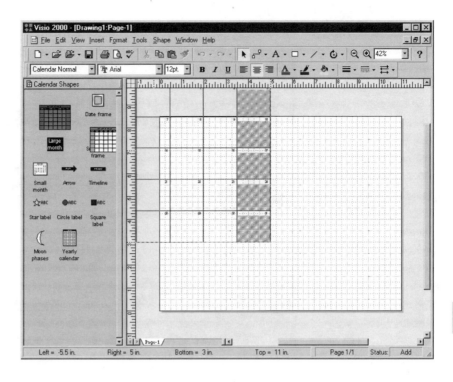

Notice that two things happen:

- You can drop the calendar shape anywhere on the page, and Visio automatically lines up the shape with the page.

- Visio displays a dialog box, which prompts you for information about the calendar.

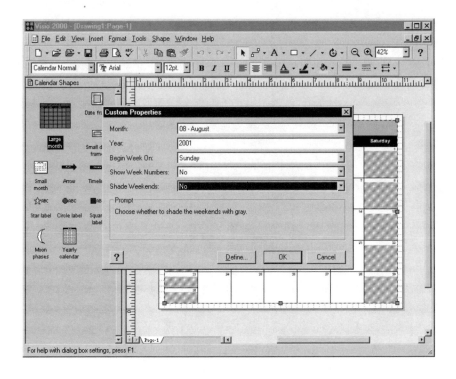

Step 6.   Fill in the information requested by the Custom Properties dialog box:

Property	Options	Default
Month	Select a month from 01-January to 12-December.	Current month
Year	Type a year, such as 2001.	Current year
Begin Week On	Select Sunday or Monday.	Sunday
Show Week Numbers	Select Yes or No.	No
Shade Weekends	Select Yes or No.	Yes

For this tutorial, specify the following options:

- Month   **08-August**
- Year   **2001**
- Begin Week On   **Sunday**
- Show Week Numbers   **No**
- Shade Weekends   **No**

Click **OK**. Notice that the calendar shows the correct dates for August 2001.

Step 7. This is a good time to save your work. From the menu bar, select **File | Save**. Notice that Visio displays the Save As dialog box. Enter a name, select a folder, and click **Save**. When the Properties dialog box appears, click **OK**. You'll find the completed drawing on the companion CD-ROM under the name Ch 3 - Month Calendar tutorial.vsd.

Step 8. To highlight certain dates, let's add some shapes to the calendar.

- Drag the **Date frame** master from the stencil onto any date square, such as day 31. Notice how the frame snaps to the square.

- Drag the **Timeline** master onto a week, such as starting on day 5. Notice how the bar snaps to the date boxes.

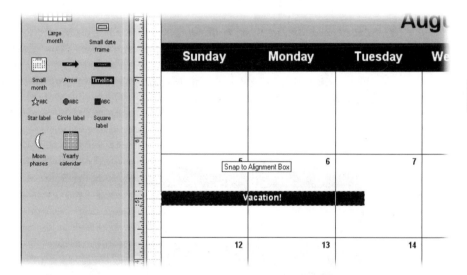

- Drag the **Moon phases** master onto the following days: 3, 11, 18, and 26. By default, all the moon shapes show the Last Quarter phase of the moon. Change three of the moon shapes, as follows: Right-click each moon shape, and select the appropriate phase from the shortcut menu. Use the following table as a guide:

Date	Moon Phase	Moon Shape
3	Full Moon	White circle
11	Last Quarter	Crescent
18	New Moon	Black circle
26	First Quarter	Crescent

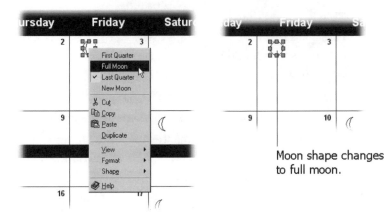

Moon shape changes
to full moon.

TIP: Changing the size of a shape   Select a shape by clicking on it. Notice the green squares that surround the timeline shape. The squares are called *handles* and allow you to change the size of the shape. The corner handles change the width and height at the same time; the end and top handles change the width and height separately.

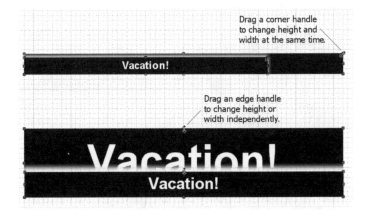

When you position the cursor over a handle, notice that the cursor changes to a double-ended arrow; this reminds you that you can move the handle in either direction. Drag the handle to change the size of the shape. Drag toward the center of the shape to make it smaller; drag away from the shape to increase its size.

In some cases, you cannot change the size of a shape. The shape is said to be *locked*. A locked shape displays gray padlocks in place of the green handles.

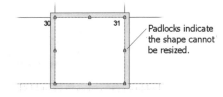

Step 9. Let's change the size of one of the shapes. Select the **Timeline** shape. Notice the green handle squares. Drag the rightmost handle to the end of the week (day 11). Notice how the shape extends itself, and that the word "Vacation" automatically centers itself.

Drag the handle to lengthen the shape.

Step 10. Let's add some notes to the calendar. Click the **A** icon on the toolbar. This is the Text tool for placing text in the drawing.

Visio allows you to place text in two ways: anywhere in the drawing and associated with a shape. We will add text to day 31, the one with the gray date frame. But first, let's select the *style* of text. From the toolbar, click the arrow next to **Calendar Normal**, and select **Calendar Day**. This text style creates larger text.

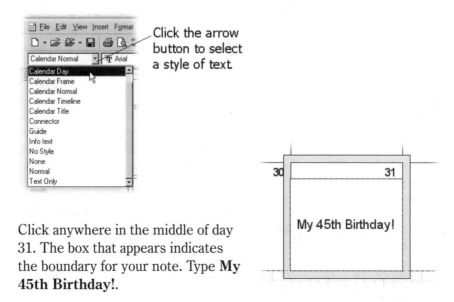

Click the arrow button to select a style of text.

Click anywhere in the middle of day 31. The box that appears indicates the boundary for your note. Type **My 45th Birthday!**.

To exit the Text tool, click the **Pointer** tool button on the toolbar (looks like a slanted black arrow).

Step 11. This completes the basic tutorial for creating a one-month calendar. The drawing should look similar to the one shown in the illustration. Remember to save the drawing (press **Ctrl+S**).

Useful Techniques

Print the Drawing

Press **Ctrl+P**. Notice the Print dialog box. If necessary, select a printer, and specify the printer's properties. When ready, click **OK**.

Close the Drawing

When you wish to close the drawing, select **File | Close** (or press **Ctrl+F4**).

Exit Visio

To exit Visio 2000, select **File | Exit** (or press **Alt+F4**).

Advanced: Making a 12-month Calendar

In this advanced tutorial, you create a 12-month calendar for next year. This involves creating a 12-page diagram.

Step 1.   With Visio still open from the basic tutorial, press **Ctrl+N**. This shortcut creates a new (blank) drawing with the existing stencil. Notice that the title bar reads "Visio 2000 - [Drawing2:Page-1]." "Drawing 2" indicates that this is the second drawing created in this session of Visio.

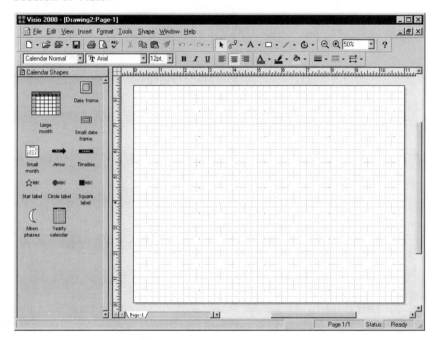

Step 2.   A new drawing contains just one page. In order for our 12-month calendar to have 12 pages, we have to add 11 pages. The procedure is somewhat laborious, because Visio does not allow you to create all pages at once. You create each new page, as follows:

■   Right-click the page tab, found under the drawing.

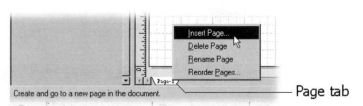

Page tab

■ From the shortcut menu, select **Insert Page**. Notice that Visio displays the Page Setup dialog box.

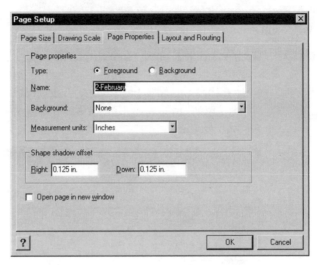

■ Change the Name to read **2-February**, and click **OK**. Notice that a new page tab appears below the drawing. It reads "2-February."

■ Repeat ten times to create pages named **3-March** through **12-December.**

■ Save your work with the **Ctrl+S** shortcut. You'll find the completed drawing on the companion CD-ROM under the name Ch 3 - Year Calendar tutorial.vsd.

TIP: Seeing all page tabs   When a drawing has more than several pages (depending on the size of the Visio window and the computer monitor), there isn't enough room to display all the page tabs. Visio displays a pair of buttons to the left of the tabs. Click the buttons to move other page tabs into view.

Click buttons to see other page tabs

Step 3.   The first page is still called "Page-1" and needs to be renamed. To rename a page, right-click its tab, and select **Rename Page.** You can edit the name of the page directly in the tab (without needing to use

the Page Setup dialog box). Change the name from Page-1 to
1-January.

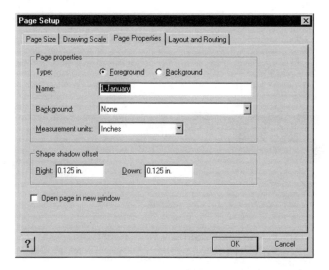

Step 4.   Add the **Large month** shape to every page. (If you need assistance
in placing the month shape on the page, review the basic tutorial.)
Remember to specify the correct name for each month. Visio does
not, unfortunately, remember any of the options you select, so you
need to specify the month and year for all 12 pages.

If after placing the month you find you've made an error, right-click
the month shape and select **Properties** from the shortcut menu.

Step 5.   You can dress up each month. For example, you can add preceding
and following months. Drag the **Small month** master onto a blank
date. Notice that the shape snaps cleanly into place. Also notice the
Custom Properties dialog box, which prompts you to specify the
month, year, and starting day of the week.

When done, press **Ctrl+S** to save your work.

Visio Resources

Visio 2000 provides the following resources for creating calendars. The templates and stencils are found in the \Visio 2000\Solutions\Project Schedule
folder.

Related Templates

Calendar.Vst

Related Stencils

Calendar Shapes.Vss

Related Toolbars

The Format Shape toolbar displays line and fill styles for modifying the look for calendar elements.

Summary

In this chapter, you learned how to place shapes and text in a diagram, then use the Custom Properties dialog box to change the shape, as well as use handles to change the shape's size. You also learned how to create additional pages in the diagram, and use the page tabs to switch between pages.

Quiz

1. Visio's Calendar solution allows you to:
    a.   Create a day planner.
    b.   Create a week planner.
    c.   Create a month planner.
    d.   Create a decade planner.

2. To change the phases of the Moon shape:
    a.   Right-click the shape and select the phase.
    b.   Drag the appropriate shape into the drawing (Full Moon shape, New Moon shape, and so on).
    c.   Phases cannot be changed.
    d.   Edit the Moon shape until it looks correct.

3. Padlocks on a shape mean it:
    a.   Cannot be erased from the diagram.
    b.   Contains copyrighted material.
    c.   Was inserted from another drawing program.
    d.   Cannot be changed in size.

4. To make a shape larger:
   a. Increase the Zoom percentage.
   b. Decrease the Zoom percentage.
   c. Drag a handle outward from the shape.
   d. Rotate a handle clockwise.

5. To place text in the diagram, select the:
   a. Word tool.
   b. Notes tool.
   c. Text tool.
   d. Paragraph tool.

6. To shorten a shape:
   a. Increase the Zoom percentage.
   b. Decrease the Zoom percentage.
   c. Drag a corner handle outward from the shape.
   d. Drag an end handle inward toward the shape's center.

7. To create a new page in the diagram:
   a. Right-click a page tab, and select Insert Page.
   b. From the menu bar, select Insert | Page.
   c. Both of the above.
   d. None of the above.

8. To rename a page:
   a. Erase the page and start over.
   b. From the menu, select Edit | Delete Page.
   c. Both of the above.
   d. None of the above.

9. When the Large month shape is dragged onto the page, it knows the current month and year.
   True / False

10. When you drag a second Large month shape onto the page, it remembers the previous month's settings.
    True / False

Lesson 3

Exercises

1. Open the Ch 2 - Month Calendar tutorial.vsd file provided on the companion CD-ROM. Right-click the calendar, and select Properties from the shortcut menu. Change the month and year for this month.

2. Open the Ch 2 - Month Calendar tutorial.vsd file provided on the companion CD-ROM. Add additional shapes and text to the calendar, such as days off school and shopping dates.

3. Create a new month calendar for next month. Add notes for important dates, like holidays and birthdays.

4. Create a mini 12-month calendar by dragging 12 copies of the Small month master onto a single page. Change the custom properties for each month. Save your work, and print it out.

5. Create a quarterly (three-month) planning calendar.

Create Business Forms

What are Business Forms?

Businesses use many different kinds of forms. Some of these forms are common, such as an invoice, order form, letterhead, and business card. Other forms are specific to a business, such as a doctor's prescription pad and a roofer's estimate sheet.

Visio 2000 does not include any "predesigned" forms beyond a business card and a fax cover sheet. Instead, Visio provides the elements needed for creating a business form—columns, check boxes, date field, borders, etc. The shapes can be used to create an invoice, order form, receipt, telephone message, and schedule.

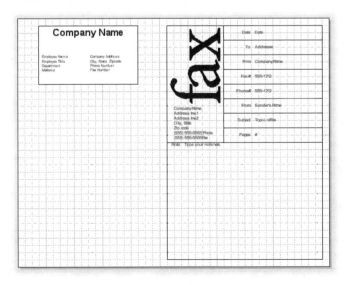

In this chapter, you learn about:

- Creating business forms, including business cards and an invoice
- Using guidelines to align shapes accurately
- Editing text
- Holding down the Ctrl key to make copies of shapes
- Using the F4 key to repeat the last command
- Displaying the page margin
- Double-clicking text for editing
- Making groups of shapes
- Applying backgrounds

Tutorials

In the following tutorials, you create a business card and an invoice.

Basic: Making a Business Card

In this basic tutorial, you quickly create a business card. There is enough room on the standard letter-size page to create ten cards. Before creating the business cards, we need to plan how to lay out ten cards on the page. Business card paper uses the following dimensions:

- Business card size   3½" wide x 2" tall
- Page size   8½" wide x 11" tall
- Top and bottom margins   ½"
- Left and right margins   ¾"

A *margin* is the area along the edges of the paper where no printing takes place. We'll use those dimensions to accurately lay out the business cards so that they print correctly on the business card paper. (The completed drawing is available on the companion CD-ROM under the name Ch 4 - Business Card tutorial.vsd.)

Step 1.   Start Visio 2000 by double-clicking its icon on the Windows Desktop. Notice the Welcome to Visio 2000 dialog box.

Step 2.   Double-click **Choose drawing type**. Notice the Choose Drawing Type dialog box.

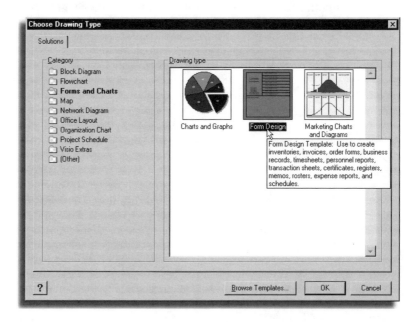

Step 3. Under Category, select **Forms and Charts**.

Step 4. In the Drawing type preview window, double-click **Form Design**. Notice that Visio opens a blank page, along with the Forms Shapes stencil on the left.

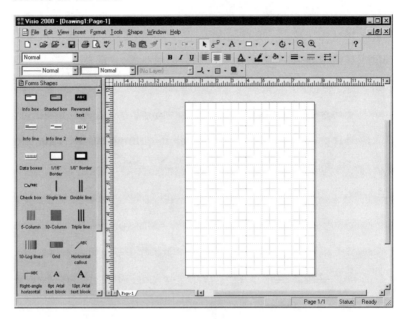

Step 5. To ensure we place the business cards accurately, we will place guidelines. The *guideline* is a horizontal or vertical line that helps us align shapes. Guidelines are displayed in the drawing, but are not printed. You create a guideline as follows:

- Ensure the rulers are displayed. If not, from the menu bar select **View | Rulers**. Notice there are two rulers: one horizontal (above the drawing page) and one vertical (to the left of the drawing page).

- Move the cursor over the horizontal ruler.

- Click and drag the cursor into the page. Notice that you are dragging a blue line; this is the guideline.

- Keep an eye on the status line. Drag the guideline until the status line reads **Y = 10.5 in.**

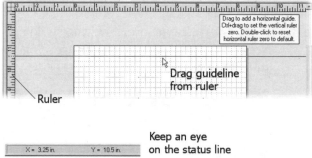

Ruler

Drag guideline
from ruler

Keep an eye
on the status line

X = 3.25 in.	Y = 10.5 in.

Step 6. Repeat to place a second horizontal guideline at **Y = 0.5 in.**

Step 7. Create two vertical guidelines by dragging them from the vertical ruler. Place them at **X = 0.75 in.** and at **X = 7.75 in.** Save your drawing.

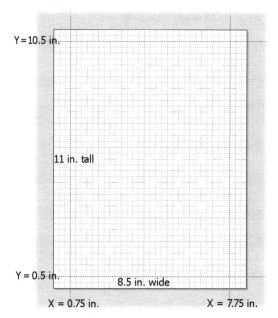

Step 8. With the guidelines in place, we can start placing the business cards. The strategy is: place one business card shape, edit the text, and make nine copies.

In the Forms Shapes stencil, drag the **Business card** master onto the page (you'll find this master in the lower half of the stencil). Drag it into the upper-left corner of the page, so that it "glues to the guides." Notice the two red squares that indicate the shape is "glued" into place. *Glue* means the shape will stay in place, attached to the guidelines. (If you were to move a guideline, the shape would move with it.)

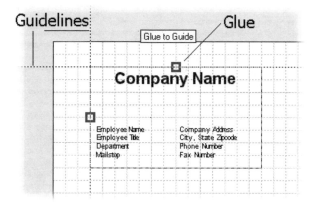

Step 9. You'll want to edit the generic text, which currently reads "Company Name," to read something else. To change the text, double-click it. Notice that the text is *highlighted* (white text on a black background). Type new text, then click anywhere else in the drawing.

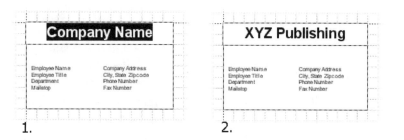

Change the other text, if you wish. Save your work with **Ctrl+S**.

Step 10. To make nine copies of the business card, make one copy to the right, then make four copies downward.

- Select the business card. Notice the green and red handles. The red handles indicate the shape is *snapped* (connected) to another shape.

- Hold down the **Ctrl** key. Notice the small plus (+) sign by the cursor, which indicates Visio will make a copy.

- Drag the card shape to the right until you see the Glue to Guide tooltip.

- Let go of the **Ctrl** key. Notice that Visio has made a copy of the business card.

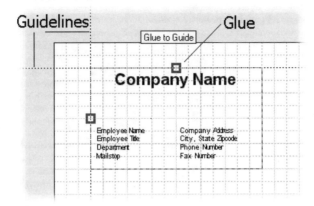

TIP: Handle colors Visio uses several forms and colors of handles to convey information about the selected shape. Note that handles only appear when one or more shapes are selected.

Handle	Meaning
Green square	First selected shape; shape can be stretched
Green circle	Shape is ready to be rotated
Green x	One-dimension shape (line)
Cyan (light blue) square	Second and subsequent selected shapes; shapes can be stretched
Small red square	Shape is snapped to another shape
Large red square	Shape is glued to another shape
Gray padlock	Shape cannot be resized

Step 11. Repeat to make two more copies below the first pair. Select both cards, hold down the **Ctrl** key, and drag downward.

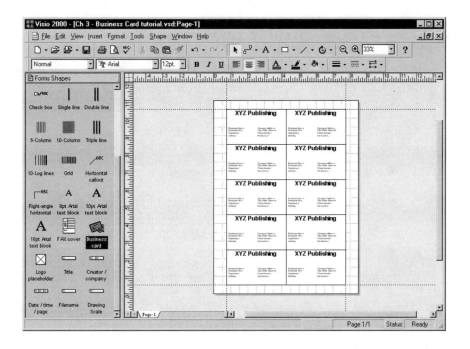

TIP: Repeating a command The function key F4 repeats the last command executed by Visio. Make use of F4 to make the final copies of the card. Simply press **F4**. Notice that Visio creates two more cards. Press **F4** twice more to place the final four business cards, for a total of ten cards in all.

Useful Techniques

Save the Drawing

Press **Ctrl+S**. Notice that Visio displays the Save As dialog box. Enter a name, select a folder, and click **Save**. When the Properties dialog box appears, click **OK**.

Print the Drawing

Press **Ctrl+P**. Notice the Print dialog box. If necessary, select a printer, and specify the printer's properties. Remember to insert the business card paper. When ready, click **OK**.

Close the Drawing

When you wish to close the drawing, select **File | Close** (from the menu bar, select **File**, then select **Close**).

Exit Visio

To exit Visio 2000, select **File | Exit**. As a shortcut, you can click the small x at the extreme right end of Visio's title bar.

Advanced: Making an Invoice Form

In this advanced tutorial, you use the shapes provided by Visio to create an invoice form. An invoice consists of several important parts:

- Your name and address
- The name and address of the person you are invoicing
- Date
- Purchase order number or other reference
- A brief description of the item being invoiced. This can include the amount, the units, the stock number, the cost per unit, and the total cost, plus additional charges, such as shipping, taxes, and discounts.
- The total amount
- Terms of payment, such as whether credit cards are accepted

Step 1.   With Visio still open from the basic tutorial, press **Ctrl+N** to create a new drawing.

Step 2.   To ensure we allow for the page margins (the unprintable edges of the paper), select **View | Page Breaks** from the menu. Notice that

Visio adds a gray border around the edges of the page. We will keep inside that border.

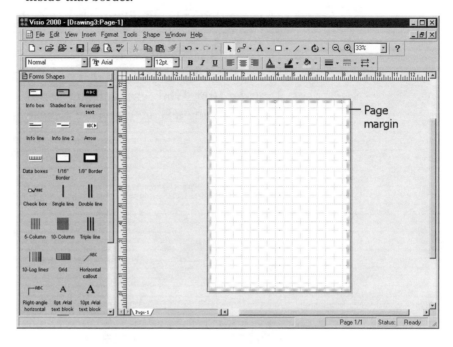

Step 3. The invoice form consists of several areas. We will create each area, then group together the shapes in each area. The illustration shows a dashed rectangle around each shape. Notice that most of the invoice consists of text and lines, with the occasional rectangle.

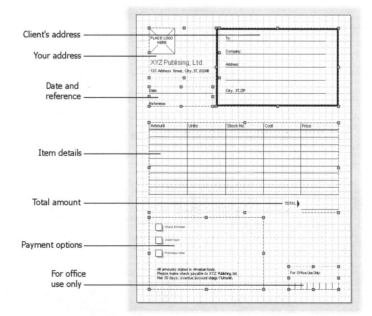

The first area we create is labeled "Your address" in the upper-left corner:

- Drag the **Logo placeholder** master from the Forms Shapes stencil onto the page. Drop the shape in the upper-left corner.
- Drag the **18pt Arial text block** master to below the logo placeholder. Later, we will edit the text with the company name.
- Drag the **10pt Arial text block** master to below the 18pt text. We will edit the text later with the company address.

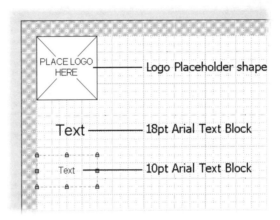

TIP: Double-clicking text In Visio, double-clicking text is a shortcut for editing text as it saves you from switching between the Text and Pointer tools.

Step 4. Here we replace the generic text:

- Double-click the larger of the two **Text** words. Notice that the text changes to reversed colors (white text with a black background; this is called *highlighted*).
- While the text is highlighted, click the **B** button (Bold) on the toolbar to "fatten up" the text.
- The text is currently centered. Click the **Align Left** button on the toolbar to left justify the text.

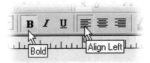

- Replace the word "Text" with "XYZ Publishing" or any other corporate name. Notice that the text *wraps around* ①. Visio fits the text into the width of the *alignment box*, the green dotted rectangle surrounding the text. We'll fix that next.

- Click outside the text block, then select the text again ②. Notice the shape has two green handles, indicating that the shape can be stretched horizontally. It also has six gray padlocks, which means the shape cannot be stretched in any other direction.

- With the cursor, drag the right handle to the right until the corporate name forms a single line ③.

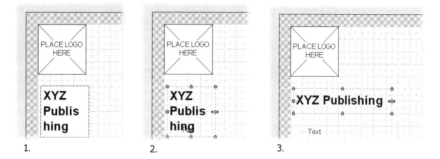

1.   2.   3.

Step 5. Repeat for the smaller "Text." Replace the generic text with the company address. If necessary, drag each of the address elements so that they line up nicely.

Step 6. We have completed the first area of the invoice. This area is your address. The three elements that make up the area—the logo, corporate name, and address—always go together. To make working with this area easier, we combine the three shapes into a *group*. In Visio, a group is a collection of shapes that act like a single shape. To collect the three shapes into a group:

- Select the three shapes by dragging a selection rectangle around the three shapes ①.

Lesson 4

- Press **Ctrl+G**, which is the shortcut to group shapes together. As an alternative, you can right-click the selected shapes, and select **Shape | Group** ②. Notice that a single alignment box surrounds the three shapes ③.

- Save your work by pressing **Ctrl+S**.

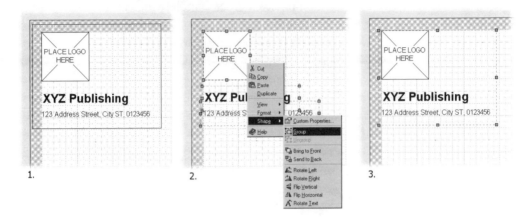

1.   2.   3.

Step 7. Complete the invoice by adding other shapes, then grouping the areas.

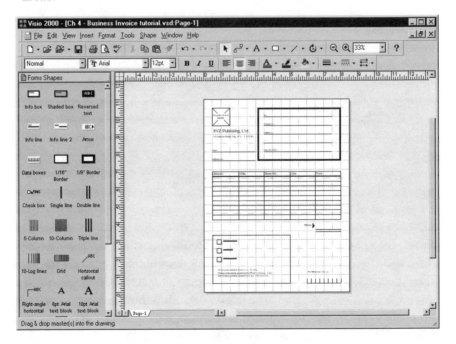

Step 8. To add some visual interest to the invoice form, you can add a background. In Visio, a *background* is a full-page graphical element that appears behind all other shapes on the page.

- Open the stencil that contains backgrounds. From the toolbar, click the down arrow next to the Open Stencil button (looks like a green folder). Select **Visio Extras | Backgrounds**. Notice that Visio opens the Background Shapes stencil.

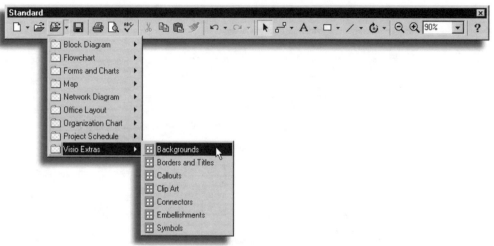

- Drag a master, such as **Background high-tech**, onto the page. Notice that Visio asks "Do you want this shape to be the background image for this page?" Click **No** to make this the background for all pages in the document. (Answering Yes makes this the background for just this page.)

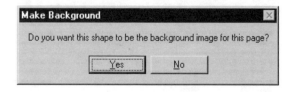

- Notice that Visio places the image behind all shapes on the page. Save your work.

Background shape

Visio Resources

Visio 2000 provides the following resources for creating business forms. The templates and stencils are found in the \Visio 2000\Solutions\Forms and Charts folder.

Related Templates

Form Design.Vst

Related Stencils

Forms Shapes.Vss

Summary

In this chapter, you learned about making business forms, including business cards and an invoice. To help you, you learned to use guidelines to align shapes accurately, and how to display the page margin, make groups of shapes, and apply background images.

You also learned about special keys, such as holding down the Ctrl key to make copies of shapes, the F4 key to repeat the last command, and double-clicking text for editing.

Quiz

1. To make a copy of a shape while dragging it, which key do you hold down?
    a. Alt
    b. Ctrl
    c. Shift
    d. Ctrl+Alt+Del

2. The purpose of function key F4 is to:
    a. Close the drawing.
    b. Exit Visio.
    c. Repeat the last command.
    d. Undo the last command.

3. Match the handle color with its meaning:
    a. Small red square   i. Second selected shape.
    b. Green square   ii. Shape is glued to another shape.
    c. Cyan square   iii. Shape is attached to another shape.
    d. Gray padlock   iv. Shape can be stretched.
    e. Large red square   v. Shape cannot be stretched.

4. To create a guideline, drag the cursor down from one of the rulers.
    True / False

5. A guideline is useful for:
    a. Printing a grid.
    b. Drawing a straight line.
    c. Learning how to use Visio.
    d. Aligning objects.

Lesson 4

6. To collect several shapes into a group:

   a. Select the shapes and press Ctrl+G.

   b. Press Ctrl+G, then select the shapes.

   c. Drag each shape on top of each other.

   d. Select shapes and type "group."

7. A background page is the last page in a diagram.
   True / False

8. Double-clicking text allows you to edit the text.
   True / False

9. On the Visio toolbar, the B button is for:

   a. Placing a shape in the background.

   b. Undoing an operation by going back.

   c. Making text bold.

   d. Inserting the letter B.

10. The alignment box is the green dotted rectangle surrounding a shape when selected.
    True / False

Exercises

1. Create a fax cover sheet by dragging the FAX cover master into a new drawing.

2. Open the Ch 4 - Business Card tutorial.vsd file found on the companion CD-ROM. Edit the text to make the business card your own.

3. Open the Ch 4 - Business Invoice tutorial.vsd file found on the companion CD-ROM. Edit the address text. Rearrange the groups to make the invoice form look different.

4. Create your own order form.

5. Create your own telephone answer pad.

Create a Flowchart

What is a Flowchart?

A *flowchart* shows relationships. For example, Visio includes a flowchart that shows how apple juice is made. Flowcharts typically consist of boxes and arrows; the boxes describe a process or decision, while the arrows indicate the direction of the flow. Businesses use many kinds of flowcharts that show how work flows through a business, how money moves through the organization, and how problems can be solved.

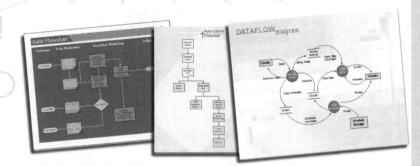

Visio is probably most commonly used for creating flowcharts. For this reason, Visio 2000 provides templates and stencils for creating many kinds of flowcharts:

In this chapter, you learn about:

- ◆ **The types of flowcharts that Visio creates**
- ◆ **Creating a flowchart with shapes that connect and number automatically**
- ◆ **Connecting shapes manually and editing connections**
- ◆ **Using the Pan & Zoom window**
- ◆ **Applying a color scheme**
- ◆ **Centering the diagram**
- ◆ **Adding hyperlinks to the diagram**
- ◆ **Bringing the diagram into PowerPoint**

Flowchart Name	Used For
Audit Diagram	Accounting, financial management, fiscal information tracking, money management, decision flowcharts, financial inventories.
Basic Flowchart	Flowcharts, top-down drawings, information tracking drawings, process planning drawings, structure prediction diagrams.
Cause and Effect Diagram	Problem-solving.
Cross-Functional Flowchart	Illustrating relationships between process and the organization.
Data Flow Diagram	Process- and data-oriented models, data flowcharts, data process diagrams, structured analysis diagrams, information flow diagrams.
IDEF0 Diagram	Model configuration management, needs and benefits analyses, requirements definitions, continuous improvement models. IDEF0 is short for "ICAM DEFinition language 0."
Mind Mapping Diagram	Mind maps for graphical representations of thought processes, brainstorming, problem-solving, rational analysis, decision making.
SDL Diagram	Communication, telecommunication systems, networks. SDL is short for "Specification and Description Language."
TQM Diagram	Business process reengineering, total quality management, continuous improvement, quality solutions. TQM is short for "Total Quality Management."
Work Flow Diagram	Information flow, automation of business processes, business process reengineering, accounting, management, human resources.

Tutorials

In the following tutorials, you create a basic flowchart, add hyperlinks, and export the flowchart to PowerPoint.

Basic: Making a Flowchart

In this basic tutorial, you quickly create a flowchart with automatic numbering. You drag and drop these symbols onto the page, then apply a color scheme to the diagram.

Step 1.   Start Visio. When the Welcome to Visio 2000 dialog box appears, double-click the **Choose drawing type** option.

Step 2. In the Choose Drawing Type dialog box, click **Flowchart**, and then double-click the **Basic Flowchart** option.

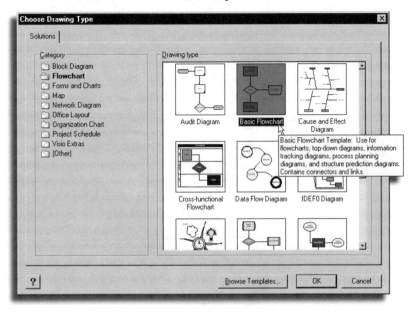

Step 3. Notice that Visio opens a new blank drawing. At the left are three stencils that hold the SmartShapes symbols: Basic Flowchart Shapes, Backgrounds, and Borders and Titles. Move the cursor over a flowchart shape in the stencil, then pause over any shape to see the shape tip.

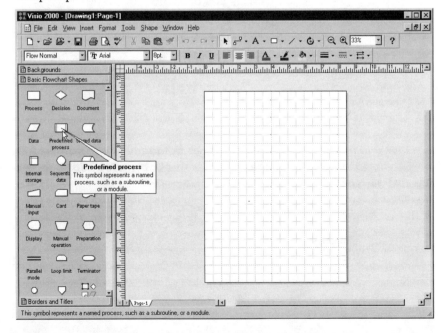

Step 4. To help draw the flowchart, select the following options for the drawing environment:

- From the menu, select **View | Windows | Pan & Zoom** ①. Notice the Pan & Zoom window ②.

- Right-click the Pan & Zoom window, and choose **AutoHide**; notice that the window slides into its title bar. (As an alternative, you can click the pushpin icon.)

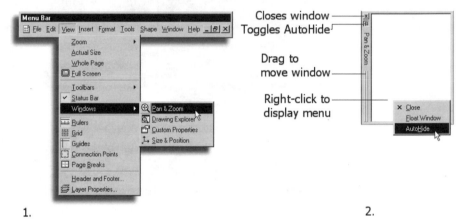

1.   2.

- On the toolbar, click the **Connector Tool** button. By selecting this tool, the shapes will connect automatically as you drag them onto the page.

TIP: Connecting shapes as you draw   Visio provides three ways to connect shapes: You can connect the shapes yourself, using connector shapes; you can have Visio connect shapes automatically as you drag shapes onto the page; and you can have Visio connect shapes after all have been placed on the page.

To have Visio connect shapes automatically as you drag them from the stencil to the page, first click the **Connector Tool** button on the Standard toolbar.

To have Visio connect shapes after all have been placed on the page, select all shapes with **Ctrl+A**. From the menu bar, select **Tools | Connect Shapes**. Notice that Visio connects shapes in the order that they were placed on the page.

TIP: Using the Pan & Zoom window   The Pan & Zoom window always shows you the entire drawing page, even when you are zoomed in. You can think of it as a road map. The heavy red rectangle shows you the zoomed in view of the page; when there is no red rectangle, the view is fully zoomed out.

- **To zoom in or out:** In the Pan & Zoom window, drag any corner or edge of the red rectangle. Make the rectangle smaller, Visio zooms in; make the rectangle larger, Visio zooms out.

- **To pan:** Place the cursor inside the red rectangle of the Pan & Zoom window. Drag the gray rectangle to a new location (the red rectangle remains in place to show you the original view).

- **To pan and zoom:** Drag the mouse outside the red rectangle. The heavy gray rectangle indicates the current view. When you release the mouse button, the gray rectangle is replaced by the red rectangle.

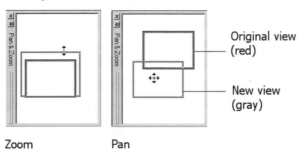

Original view (red)

New view (gray)

Zoom   Pan

Step 5.   Visio 2000 is able to automatically number shapes as you drag them into the drawing. (You can, if you prefer, number the shapes after you place them in the drawing.) To turn on automatic numbering, from the menu, choose **Tools | Number Shapes.** When the Number Shapes dialog box appears, select the following options:

- Operation   **Auto Number**
- Apply To   **All Shapes**
- Continue numbering   ✓ (on: check mark shows)
  shapes as dropped on page
- Start with   1
- Interval   1
- Preceding Text   **<none>**

Click **OK** to dismiss the dialog box.

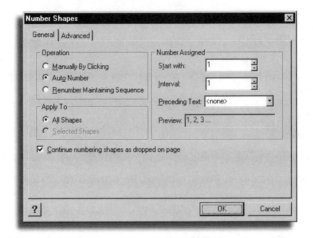

Step 6. With the preparation out of the way, let's create a flowchart. From the Basic Flowchart Shapes stencil, drag the **Process** master onto the page. Notice that the shape contains the number "1" in its center.

Step 7. Repeat Step 6, this time dragging the **Data** master onto the page. As you position it below the Process shape, notice how the dashed lines help you position one shape precisely below the other. You know the two shapes are aligned when you see the Snap to Dynamic Grid tooltip.

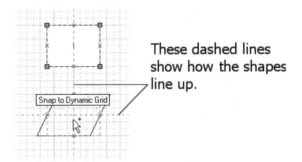

These dashed lines show how the shapes line up.

Step 8. Continue dragging masters onto the page. Notice how Visio automatically connects and numbers them. You can discontinue the automatic numbering at any time by right-clicking the page (not a shape) and selecting **Number Shapes on Drop**.

TIP: Quickly changing the format of all text   If you find the size of the numbers to be too small, here is how to quickly change the format of all text on a page:

- Press **Ctrl+A** to select everything on the page.

- From the toolbar, select a new font size, such as 24. Notice that Visio changes the size of all text to the new size.

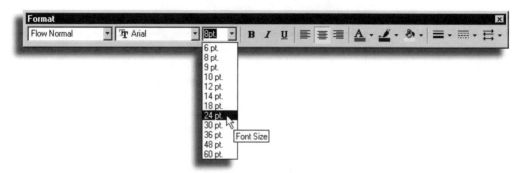

The Font Size list box lists the commonly used sizes, ranging from 6pt to 60pt. *Pt* is short for "point," which is a unit of measurement used by typographers and printers. There are 72 points to the inch (strictly speaking, it's actually 72.727272...). Thus, a font size of 72pt creates text that is 1" (or 2.5cm) tall. A font size of 6pt is 1/12" (or 2.1mm) tall.

You are not limited to the points listed in the Font Size list box. You may type any value you like, such as 144 for 2-inch tall text, or 1 for microscopic text that is a mere 0.01" tall.

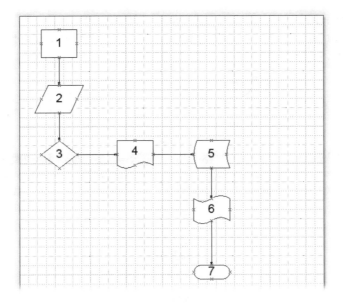

Step 9. This flowchart is black and white. Visio allows you change its colors instantly using *color schemes*, predefined colors for lines and fills. To change the color scheme, follow these steps:

- Right-click the page (not a shape or connector).
- From the shortcut menu, select **Color Schemes.**

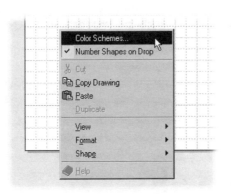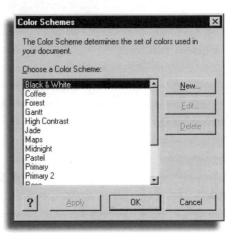

- Choose a color scheme name from the list. (You can create a new color scheme by clicking the **New** button.)
- To get an idea of what it will look like, click **Apply.**

Click **OK.**

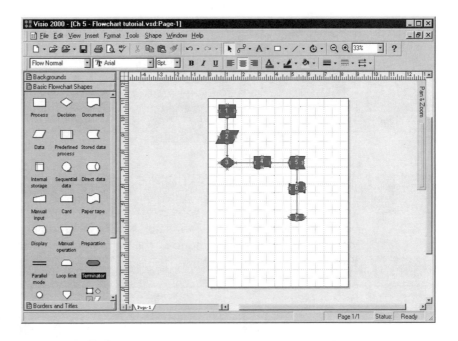

Step 10. To add a branch to the flowchart, such as at the Decision diamond (shape #3), perform the following steps:

Turn off the Connection tool by clicking the **Pointer** tool button on the toolbar. As an alternative, you can press **Ctrl+1** (that's number one, not letter I).

- Drag a master onto the page, such as the Process shape.
- Select the **Decision** shape. Notice the green selection handles.
- Hold down the **Ctrl** key, and select the **Process** shape. Notice the cyan (light blue) selection handles.
- From the menu, select **Tools | Connect Shapes**. Notice that Visio draws a connector, with the arrow pointing to the Process shape.

TIP: Selection order is important!   You can use this method to connect two or more shapes at a time. The important thing to remember is that Visio starts with the first-selected shape, then places connectors between shapes in the order that you picked them.

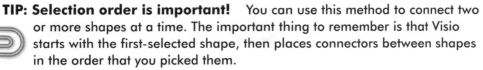

Lesson **5**

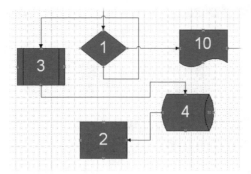

Visio attempts to route the connectors as best it can, but the result may not be pretty. You can edit the connector's route by dragging a vertex, which looks like a tiny green diamond at the bend of a connector ①. Notice that Visio reroutes the connector ②.

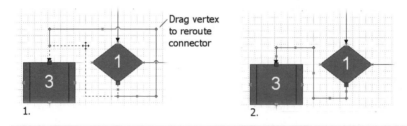

Useful Techniques

To Move a Shape

Select the shape ①. Notice the green handles, which indicate the shape is selected.

Drag the shape to the new location ②. Notice that the connector automatically follows along ③.

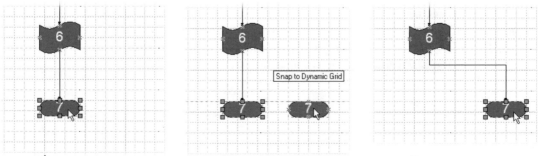

To Copy a Shape

Select the shape and hold down the **Ctrl** key (think of the "C" in both Ctrl and Copy to remind you that holding down Ctrl copies the shape). Notice the plus sign (+) next to the cursor; this is to remind you the shape is being copied. Drag the shape to the new location. Notice that the connector does <u>not</u> follow along.

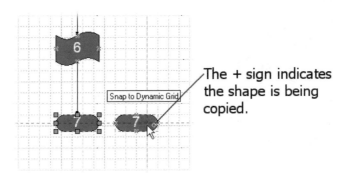

The + sign indicates the shape is being copied.

To Renumber Shapes

In the basic tutorial, you turned on automatic numbering. If you want to renumber the shapes or change the numbering scheme, select from the menu **Tools | Number Shapes**. In the Number Shapes dialog box, make changes (optional), select **Renumber Maintaining Sequence**, and click **OK**.

To Edit Text in a Shape

Double-click the shape ①. Notice that the text is highlighted (white text on a black background). Edit the text ②, then click anywhere else on the page ③.

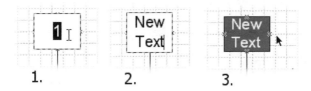

1.   2.   3.

To Add a Border

Click the header of the Borders and Titles stencil ①, and drag a border master from the stencil onto the page. Notice that the border automatically positions itself on the page ②. Edit the "Title/Company Name" text; notice that Visio automatically inserts today's date.

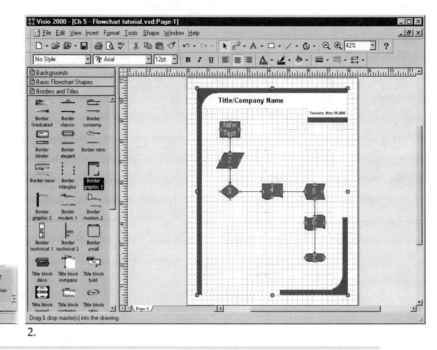

1.   2.

TIP: Centering the diagram   Before adding a border, you may want to center the diagram on the page. This ensures that the border lines and text don't overrun your diagram. To center the diagram, from the menu bar select **Tools | Center Drawing**.

Advanced: Creating a Hyperlinked Flowchart

In this advanced tutorial, you add hyperlinks between a Visio drawing and a Word document, and export the flowchart diagram to PowerPoint.

Step 1.   Ensure that Visio is open with the diagram you created in the basic tutorial. If necessary, you can open the Ch 5 - Flowchart tutorial.vsd file from the companion CD-ROM included with this book.

Step 2.   Visio 2000 allows you to add one (or more) hyperlinks to any shape on the page, or to the page itself. Here we add the hyperlink to a shape. Although you can add the hyperlink to any shape, it can be more convenient to use a shape specifically designed for the purpose. From the Borders and Titles stencil, drag the **Hyperlink Circle 1** master onto the page.

Step 3.   Notice that Visio displays the Custom Properties dialog box, which allows you to change the look of the icon. Click the down arrow next to Home, and select **Info**. Click **OK**.

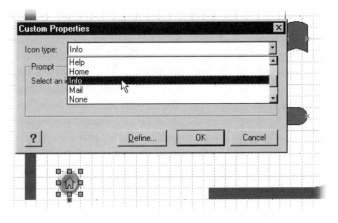

Step 4. Notice the Hyperlinks dialog box.

The various fields have the following meaning:

Address: The path and filename of the hyperlinked file. The file may be located on your computer, or on another computer connected to yours via a local network or the Internet. The address is also known as the *URL* (short for Uniform Resource Locator, the universal file naming system used by the Internet). The easy way to specify the full path is to click the **Browse** button, then select the **Internet Address** or **Local File** options.

Sub-address: A location within the file. In the case of a Visio drawing, this can be a specific page or shape. In the case of a Web site, this is usually an *anchor*.

Description: (Optional) When this is filled in, Visio displays the description instead of the address or URL.

Use relative path for hyperlink: A *relative path* describes the path to the hyperlinked file relative to either the Visio drawing or the path set in the Summary tab of the Properties dialog box (from the menu, select **File | Properties**). The drawback to using a relative path is that the hyperlink is lost if either file is moved.

When this option is turned off, Visio uses the *absolute path*. The benefit is that you can move the Visio file without breaking the hyperlink; the hyperlink is still broken, however, if the hyperlinked file is moved.

New: Adds another address to the list. This allows a single shape (or page) to provide access to more than one hyperlink.

Delete: Removes the selected address from the list.

Default: When there is more than one address, selects the address that will appear by default.

Enter the following information:

Address: Click **Browse**, then **Local File**. Select the **Ch 3 - Year Calendar tutorial.vsd** file, since it is a multi-page drawing.

Sub-address: Click **Browse**. Notice that the second Hyperlink dialog box has three options:

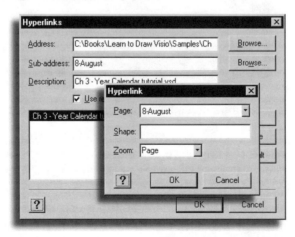

- **Page**: Select a page name, such as **8-August**.
- **Shape**: Allows you to specify the name of a shape on the page. Visio does not, however, list the names of the shapes in the page. Leave blank.
- **Zoom**: Select the **Page** zoom level.

Click **OK** twice to dismiss both dialog boxes.

Step 5. Pass the cursor over the hyperlinked shape. Notice that the cursor changes shape, and that a tooltip describes the name of the hyperlink.

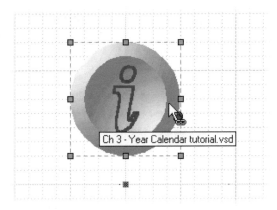

TIP: Editing hyperlinks To edit a hyperlink, select the shape and press **Ctrl+K** (or select **Insert | Hyperlinks** from the menu bar).

Step 6. To go to the hyperlinked file, right-click the shape and select the address from the shortcut menu. Notice that Visio displays the "Ch 3 - Year Calendar tutorial" drawing and "8-August" page.

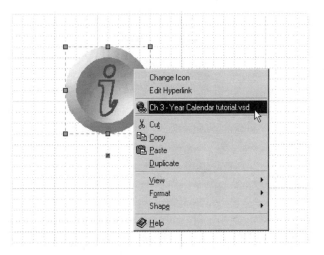

Step 7. There are several ways to get back to the original drawing. One method is to select from the menu bar **Windows |** *filename*, as shown in the following illustration.

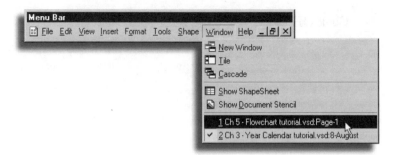

Another method is to press **Ctrl+Tab**, which switches between the various drawings open in Visio.

If you will be hyperlinking between documents in Visio and other applications, it makes more sense to use the Web toolbar. To open the Web toolbar, right-click any toolbar and select **Web** ①. Notice the Web toolbar ②. The two arrow icons move you back and forth between hyperlinked files.

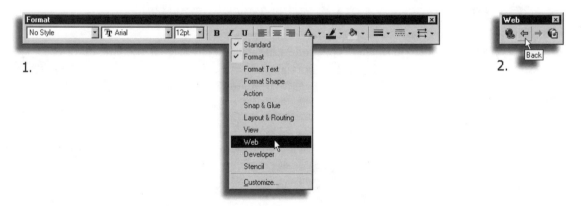

Step 8. In a similar manner, you can link Visio diagrams to other documents. For example, in a Word document select **Insert | Hyperlink**. In the Insert Hyperlink dialog box, click **Browse**, then select the name of a Visio drawing. You can optionally include the name of a Visio page.

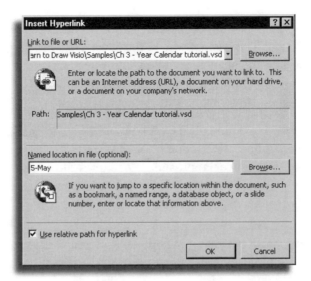

After you click **OK**, Word displays the hyperlink as underlined blue text.

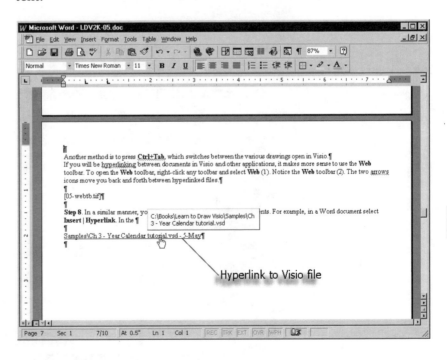

Hyperlink to Visio file

When you click the hyperlink, Visio is launched automatically with the drawing, displaying the correct page.

Step 9. You may want to include your flowchart in PowerPoint for presentation. The easiest way to display a Visio drawing in PowerPoint is to drag the shapes, as follows:

- Open PowerPoint, and insert a new slide.
- In Visio, press **Ctrl+A** to select all shapes on the page.
- Hold down the **Ctrl** key, and drag the shapes to the PowerPoint slide. (If you don't hold down the Ctrl key, the shapes are <u>moved</u> to PowerPoint, and erased from the Visio drawing. If this happens, simply click the **Undo** button in Visio to bring back the shapes.)

TIP: Reversing your actions When you find you made a mistake, press **Ctrl+Z**. As an alternative, you can click the **Undo** button on the toolbar. Visio 2000 reverses your mistake. You can press **Ctrl+Z** several times to undo several mistakes. Think of undo as your best friend.

You can also "undo" the undo. This is called "redo." Press **Ctrl+Y** (or click the **Redo** button on the toolbar) to reverse the effect of the undo.

- Notice the diagram in PowerPoint. It may be necessary to resize the diagram to fit the slide.

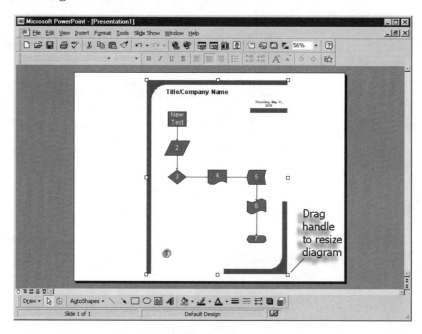

Step 10. To edit the diagram within PowerPoint, double-click the Visio diagram. Notice two things: the diagram appears in a Visio window, and the Visio menu bar and toolbars replace those of PowerPoint.

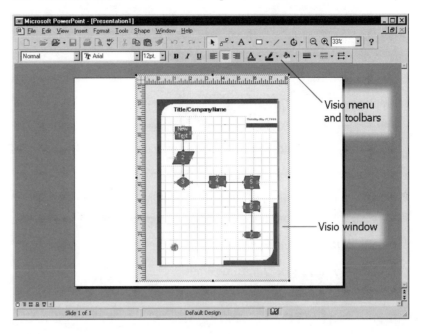

Visio Resources

Visio 2000 provides the following resources for creating flowcharts. The templates and stencils are found in the \Visio 2000\Solutions\Flowchart folder.

Related Templates

Audit Diagram.Vst
Basic Flowchart.Vst
Cause and Effect Diagram.Vst
Cross-functional Flowchart.Vst
Data Flow Diagram.Vst
IDEF0 Diagram.Vst
Mind Mapping.Vst
SDL Diagram.Vst
TQM Diagram.Vst
Work Flow Diagram.Vst

Lesson 5

Related Stencils

Miscellaneous Flowchart Shapes.Vss

Audit diagrams:

Audit Diagram Shapes.Vss

Basic flowcharts:

Basic Flowchart Shapes.Vss

Cause and effect diagrams:

Cause and Effect Shapes.Vss

Cross-functional flowcharts:

Cross-functional Flowchart Shapes Horizontal.Vss
Cross-functional Flowchart Shapes Vertical.Vss

Data flow diagrams:

Data Flow Diagram Shapes.Vss

IDEF0 diagrams:

IDEF0 Diagram Shapes.Vss

Mind mapping:

Mind Mapping Shapes.Vss

SDL diagram:

SDL Diagram Shapes.Vss

TQM diagrams:

TQM Diagram Shapes.Vss

Work flow diagrams:

Work Flow Diagram Shapes.Vss

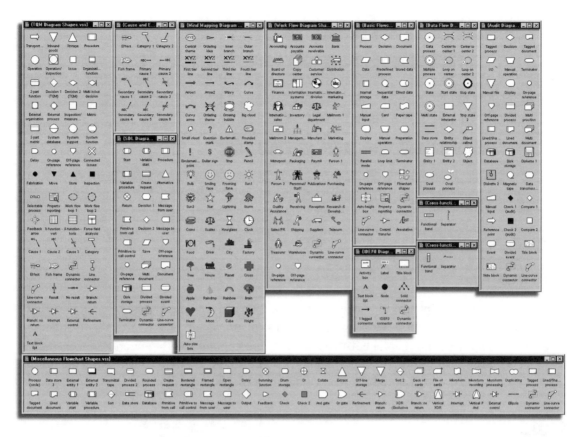

Related Commands and Wizards

Tools | Color Schemes

Color schemes are applied to underlying styles in the diagram. Any shape that uses styles based on underlying styles changes automatically. Color schemes are useful for making a diagram more legible, and to apply company-wide standards. For example, you can use the Black & White scheme (found in the Color Schemes dialog box) to temporarily convert the diagram to monochrome colors (no shades of gray), which produces a more legible laser printout.

Visio 2000 includes color schemes for the following solutions: Audit Diagram, Basic Diagram, Basic Flowchart, Basic Network, Block Diagram, Block Diagram With Perspective, Calendar, Cause and Effect Diagram, Charts and Graphs, Cross-Functional Flowchart, Data Flow Diagram, Form Design, Gantt Chart, Geographic Maps, IDEF0 Diagram, Marketing Charts and Diagrams, Mind Mapping, Organization Chart, Organization Chart Wizard, PERT Chart, SDL Diagram, Timeline, TQM Diagram, and Work Flow Diagram.

Tools | Number Shapes

Shapes can be numbered manually, automatically, or as you drag them onto the page. This command displays a dialog box that provides many options, such as the number to start with, the interval, prefix text, and number placement, as well as allowing toggling the visibility of the text.

Import Flowchart Data Wizard

This wizard takes you through the steps needed to import flowchart data from a plain text file (*.txt) or an Excel spreadsheet file (*.xls). It even assists you in creating the TXT and XLS files. To start this wizard, from the menu bar select **Tools | Macros | Flowcharts | Import Flowchart Data Wizard**.

Summary

In this chapter, you learned about creating a simple flowchart with shapes that connect and number automatically. You also learned how to edit the shape text and the connections between shapes. You applied a color scheme to the diagram, centered the diagram on the page, and added hyperlinks to the diagram. Finally, you dragged the Visio diagram into a PowerPoint slide.

Quiz

1. The Connector tool connects shapes automatically as they are dragged onto the page.

   True / False

2. Once numbered automatically, Visio cannot renumber shapes.

   True / False

3. When measuring the height of text, 1 pt (one point) is equal to:

   a. 1 inch.

   b. 1/100 inch.

   c. 1/72 inch.

   d. 1/72 meter.

4. Match the shortcut key with its meaning:

   a. Ctrl+A   i.   Pointer tool.

   b. Ctrl+1   ii.   Insert or Edit Hyperlinks.

   c. Ctrl+drag   iii.   Select All.

   d. Ctrl+K   iv.   Switch to another drawing in Visio.

e. Ctrl+Tab   v.   Copy shapes.

5. When handles are green, it means:
    a. The shape can be moved.
    b. The shape is the first selected shape.
    c. The shape can be stretched.
    d. All of the above.

6. The purpose of a hyperlink is:
    a. To compress the size of the diagram.
    b. To link to another file or an Internet location.
    c. To expand the diagram's shapes.
    d. To examine the shape's ShapeSheet.

7. Visio can hyperlink to a specific page in another Visio file.
    True / False

8. The purpose of a color scheme is to:
    a. Change the color of all shapes at once.
    b. Change the color of the Visio user interface.
    c. Specify a unique color.
    d. Create a 3-D look for shapes.

9. The quick way to add or edit text in a shape is:
    a. Right-click the shape, and select Edit Text.
    b. From the menu bar, select Format | Text.
    c. Double-click the shape.
    d. Single-click the shape.

10. A shape can have more than one hyperlink.
    True / False

Exercises

1. Open the Ch 5 - Flowchart tutorial.vsd file from the companion CD-ROM. Select the Connector tool, and drag five more shapes onto the page.

2. Open a document in another application, such as Word, and create a hyperlink to a Visio drawing.

3. Create a flowchart from scratch. Include a minimum of six shapes. Use the automatic connection and numbering features.

4. Re-create the flowchart shown in the illustration below.

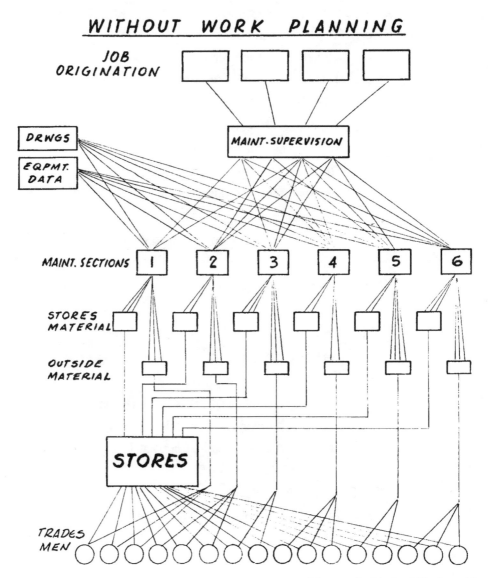

Diagram by Herbert Grabowski

5. Re-create the flowchart shown in the illustration below.

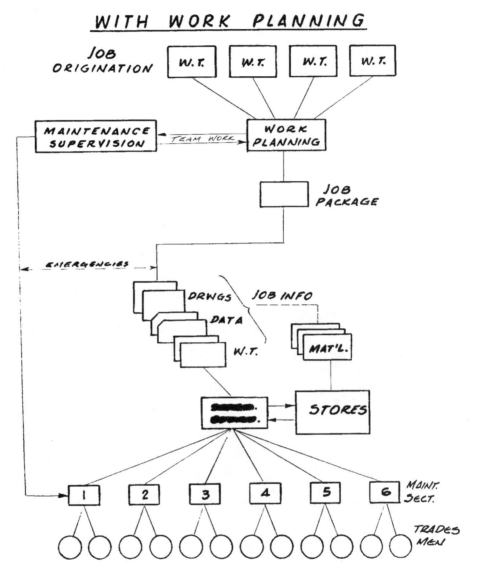

Diagram by Herbert Grabowski

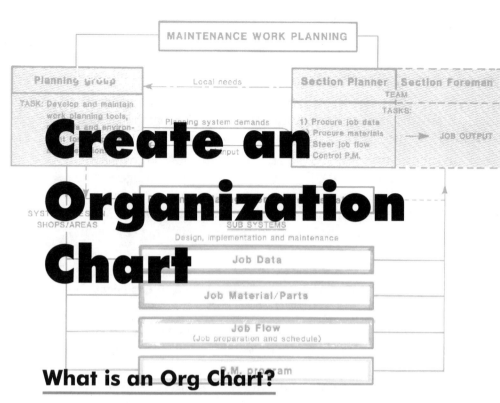

Create an Organization Chart

In this chapter, you learn about:

◆ **Creating an organization chart in two ways: dragging shapes onto the page and from data stored in a file**

◆ **Editing the chart's contents, including changing the look of the chart**

◆ **Creating a multi-page org chart**

◆ **Viewing and editing custom properties**

◆ **Comparing the differences between two similar org charts**

What is an Org Chart?

Org is short for "organization." An org chart shows the organization of personnel in a company. Visio Standard 2000's strongest feature is its Organization Chart solution. It allows you to easily create simple and complex org charts:

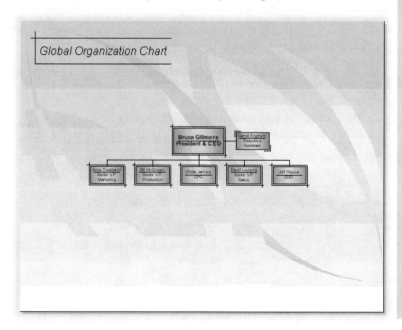

- Quickly create an org chart by dragging staff shapes onto manager shapes; Visio automatically orients and connects the shapes appropriately.

- To handle very large org charts, you can place departments on separate pages; Visio synchronizes the charts between pages. From the menu bar, select Organization Chart | Create Synchronized Copy.

- Visio can automatically generate an org chart from tab- and comma-delimited text (.txt), Org Plus (.txt), Excel (.xls), Microsoft Exchange Server Directory, and a file created by an Open Database Connectivity (ODBC)-compliant database application. From the menu bar, select File | New | Organization Chart | Organization Chart Wizard to start the Organization Chart Wizard.

- Visio can update an older org chart by comparing it with a newer version. From the menu bar, select Organization Chart | Compare Organization Data.

- Visio lets you quickly change the layout, without needing to manually move shapes. Select the primary shape, then from the menu bar select Organization Chart | Lay Out Subordinates.

- Instantly change the appearance of the org chart by using predefined styles and color schemes. From the menu bar, select Organization Chart | Options | Org Chart Theme and Tools | Color Schemes.

Tutorials

In the following tutorials, you draw a multi-page organization chart, then use one of Visio's wizards to create an org chart from a data file.

Basic: Making an Org Chart

In this basic tutorial, you quickly create a multi-page organization chart, or *org chart* for short. In this tutorial, you see the tools provided by Visio 2000 to make org chart creation easier.

Step 1.   Start Visio. When the Welcome to Visio 2000 dialog box appears, double-click the **Choose drawing type** option.

Step 2.   In the Choose Drawing Type dialog box, click **Organization Chart**, and then double-click the **Organization Chart** option.

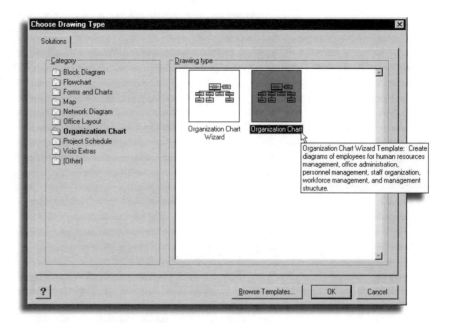

Step 3. Notice that Visio opens a new blank drawing. At the left are three stencils that hold the SmartShapes symbols: Organization Chart Shapes, Backgrounds, and Borders and Titles. The page is in landscape orientation, meaning that it is wider than tall.

Notice, too, that Visio displays the Organization Chart toolbar, as well as the Organization Chart item on the menu bar. These contain commands specific to creating org charts, which we will work with later in this tutorial.

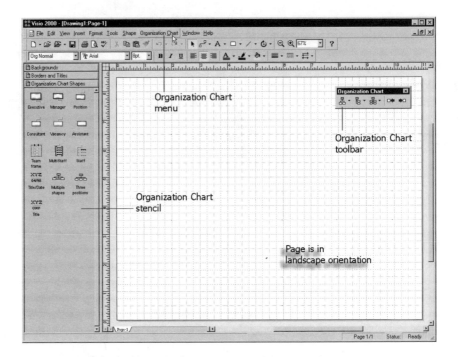

Step 4. Drag the **Executive** master from the Organization Chart Shapes stencil onto the upper-center of the page.

Step 5. Drag the **Manager** master from the stencil ①. This is important: Drop the shape on the Executive shape ②. Notice that Visio automatically positions the Manager shape below the Executive shape, and connects the two ③.

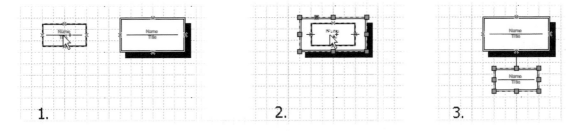

Step 6. Repeat Step 5: Drag the **Manager** master from the stencil on top of the Executive shape. Notice that Visio makes room to evenly position both Manager shapes under the Executive shape.

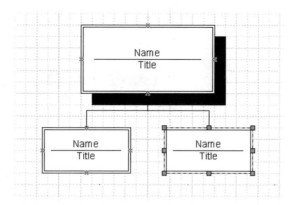

Step 7.   Drag the **Assistant** master from the stencil, and drop it on the Executive shape. Notice that Visio places the shape to the right of the Executive shape.

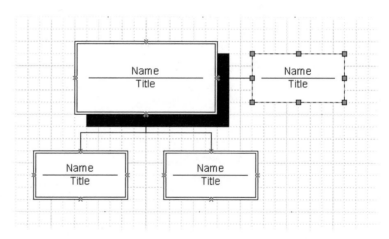

Step 8.   Drag a **Position** master on top of the left-hand Manager master. Repeat. Notice the two Position shapes below the Manager shape.

Visio has a faster method for adding multiple positions. Drag the **Multiple Shapes** master on top of the right-hand Manager shape. Notice the Add Multiple Shapes dialog box.

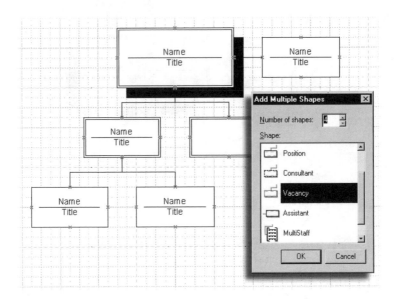

Step 9.   In the Add Multiple Shapes dialog box, select the following options:

- Number of shapes   **4**
- Shape   **Vacancy**

Click **OK**. Notice that Visio adds a "ladder" of four blank boxes.

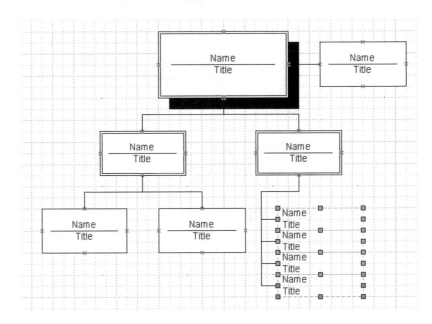

Step 10. Drag the **Title/Date** master to the top of the page. Notice that Visio provides today's date automatically. Double-click the "Company Name" text to edit it.

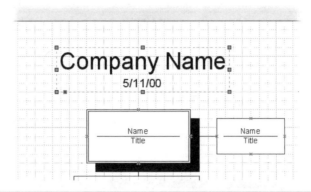

TIP: Hiding subordinate shapes To hide subordinate shapes, from the menu select **Organization Chart | Hide Subordinates**. Notice that all shapes, except the topmost shape, disappear.

To reveal the hidden subordinates, from the menu select **Organization Chart | Show Subordinates**. Notice that the shapes reappear.

Step 11. When your org chart gets too large for a single page, you can employ several strategies:

Strategy 1: Squeeze the boxes together. From the menu bar, select **Organization Chart | Change Layout Spacing**. In the Layout Spacing dialog box, click the **Spacing** button. Make changes, then click the **Apply** button to see the effect of your change. Click **OK** when satisfied with the arrangement.

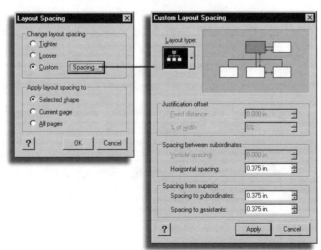

Strategy 2: Make the boxes smaller. From the menu bar, select **Organization Chart | Options**. In the Options dialog box, specify a smaller box size. Making a box 67% smaller (0.67" wide, instead of 1" wide) makes its area 50% smaller. You may also need to reduce the size of the text: press **Ctrl+A** to select all objects, then specify a smaller font size.

Strategy 3: Make the page larger. From the menu bar, select **File | Page Setup**. In the **Page Size** tab, select a larger size from the Pre-defined size list, such as "Legal: 14 in. x 8.5 in." When it comes time to print the page, you must either print to a printer that can handle the larger page size, or scale the page to fit a standard 8½" x 11" sheet.

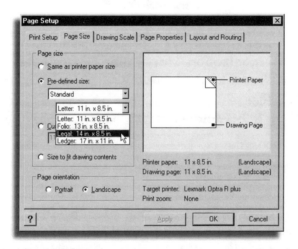

Strategy 4: Continue on another page. Visio is able to maintain synchronized pages for very large org charts. *Synchronized* means that if a change occurs in one page, it is reflected in affected pages. To create a synchronized page, select the shape that will be the superior shape on the synchronized page. For the purposes of this tutorial, use the left-hand Manager shape. Right-click the **Manager** shape, and select **Create Synchronized Copy** ① from the shortcut menu.

Notice the Create Synchronized Copy dialog box ②. Specify the following options, then click **OK**:

■ Create a synchronized copy on   **New page**

■ Hide subordinates on original page   ✓ (turned on)

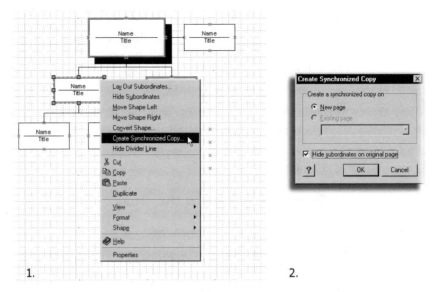

1.

2.

Notice that Visio creates a new page (called "Page-2") with the Manager shape and its two subordinates. Click the **Page-1** tab to see what happened on the original page. Notice the Manager shape looks like a stack of rectangles. Right-click the shape, and select **Show Subordinates**. Visio displays the subordinate shapes, which are the same ones shown on Page-2. Make a change to the text of one subordinate shape: Change "Name | Title" to "Super Dave | Understudy." Click the **Page-2** tab, and notice that the change is reflected on the synchronized page.

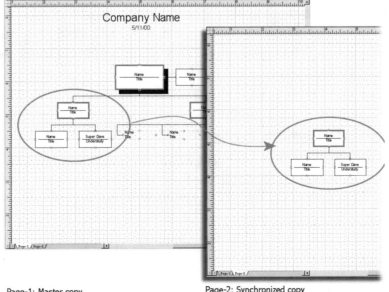

Page-1: Master copy

Page-2: Synchronized copy

> **TIP: Synchronization limitations**   To ensure the pages stay synchronized, you may only add shapes by dragging from the stencil to on top of a superior shape. You cannot use **Ctrl**+drag or the clipboard (**Ctrl+C** and **Ctrl+V**) to make copies.

Step 12.   Save your work by pressing **Ctrl+S**. This diagram can be found on the companion CD-ROM under Ch 6 - Org 1 chart tutorial.vsd.

Useful Techniques

To Change the Text in the Boxes

Double-click a shape, and edit the text.

To Change the Type of Shape

Right-click the shape, and select **Convert Shape** ①. From the Convert Shape dialog box, select a new shape type ②, and click **OK**.

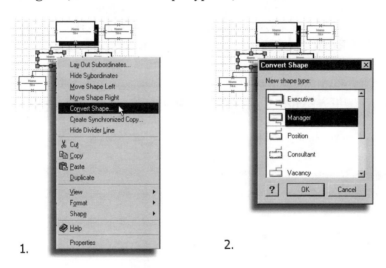

1.   2.

To Change the Look of the Org Chart

From the menu bar, select **Organization Chart | Options**. In the Options dialog box, select a different name from the Org Chart Theme list. Click **OK**.

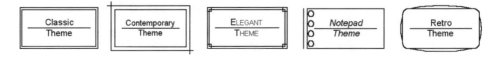

To Find a Person in the Org Chart

In a small organization chart, it is easy to find a person. But when the chart is large or spans more than one page, finding a name is harder. Visio has a tool that helps you do this. From the menu bar, select **Organization Chart | Find Person**. In the Find Person dialog box, enter the person's name in the Find what field. Click **Find Next**.

To Change the Layout of the Chart

Select the topmost shape (Visio calls this the *superior* shape). On the Organization Chart toolbar, select the **Horizontal Layout**, **Vertical Layout**, or **Side-by-side Layout** button. Notice the flyout that presents options. Select an option, and notice how the layout rearranges itself.

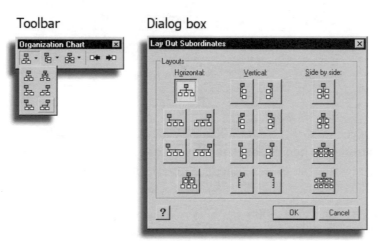

As an alternative: select the superior shape. From the menu, select **Organization Chart | Lay Out Subordinates**. Make your selection from the Lay Out Subordinates dialog box, and click **OK**.

Lesson

Advanced: Creating an Org Chart from a Data File

In this tutorial, you learn how to have Visio create a diagram automatically from data stored in a file. You also learn how to create a new custom property, and compare the differences between two org charts.

The data that defines an org chart can be stored in a spreadsheet file, a plain text (ASCII) file, in database records, or in an Exchange Server directory. Examples of the spreadsheet and text files are illustrated below.

To help you import the data, Visio provides a wizard that takes you through the steps needed to import the data. The wizard prompts you for the data in two forms: stored in an existing file or entered while the wizard is running. In this tutorial, you work with a file provided on the companion CD-ROM.

Step 1.   Start Visio 2000. (If Visio is already running, then from the menu bar select **File | New | Choose Drawing Type**.) When the Welcome to Visio 2000 dialog box appears, double-click the **Choose drawing type** option.

Step 2.   In the Choose Drawing Type dialog box, select **Organization Chart**. Then select **Organization Chart Wizard**, and click **OK**.

Step 3. When the Organization Chart Wizard appears, ensure that the **Information that's already stored in a file or database** option is selected. Click **Next**.

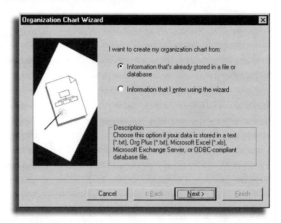

Step 4. Ensure that the **A text, Org Plus (.txt), or Microsoft Excel file** option is selected, and click **Next**.

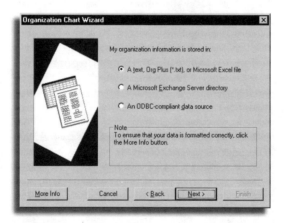

Step 5. Click **Browse**. Notice the file dialog box. Locate the Ch 6 - Org Chart Data.xls file on the companion CD-ROM. Click **Open**, then click **Next**.

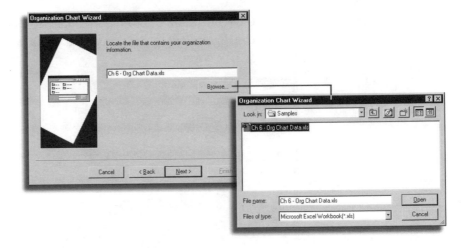

Step 6.   Ensure that the fields correctly match the data. Visio attempts to automatically match its field names (in the left column) with field names found in the data file (right column). The list boxes in the right column list the names found in the *header* line (the first line in the data file).

- Name   **Name**
- Reports to   **Reports_To**
- First name (optional)   **<none>**

Click **Next**.

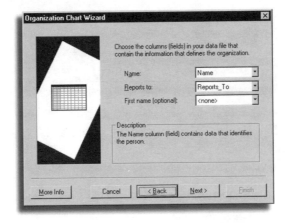

Step 7.   Each org shape can display two lines of text. In most cases, the shape contains the name of the person and their title. Here you specify the data to display in the org shapes. Again, Visio lists the names found in the header line of the data file. For this tutorial, select the following:

- First line   **Name**
- Second line   **Position**

Click **Next**.

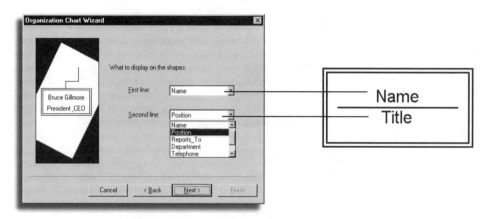

Step 8. Although each org shape displays just two pieces of data (the full name and the title), additional data can be stored in custom properties (we see these later in the tutorial). Select all entries in Data File Columns:

Hold down the **Shift** key, and select **Name**, the first item in the list. Select **E-Mail**, the second to last item in the list. Notice that Visio highlights all items, except Master_Shape, which contains no data. Click **Add**. Notice that all items now appear under Custom Property fields. Click **Next**.

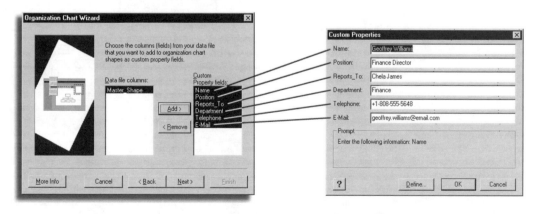

Step 9. Ensure the **I want the wizard to automatically break my organization chart across pages** option is selected. Click **Finish**.

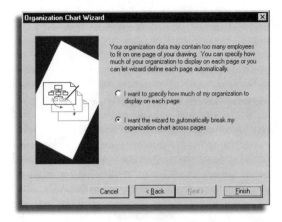

It takes Visio a minute or two to create the org chart automatically from the data stored in the spreadsheet file.

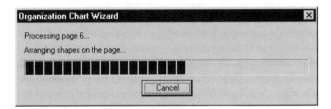

When done, the org chart is ten pages long. If you wish, save the drawing. It can be found under Ch 6 - Org 2 chart tutorial.vsd on the companion CD-ROM.

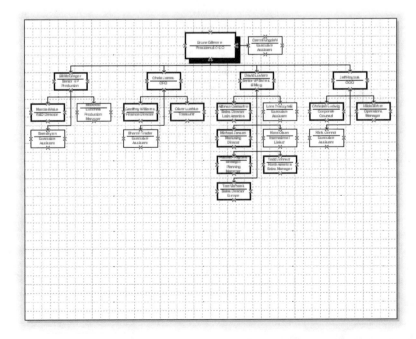

Step 10. Each shape in this org chart displays a name and a title. Earlier in Step 8, I mentioned that there was more data stored in *custom properties*. Each shape in this drawing has custom properties that you can change, but not all shapes in other drawings necessarily have custom properties.

Custom properties allow you to attach your own data to a shape. This can be the inventory number of a chair, the user name of a computer, or the flow characteristics of a pipe. Custom properties make Visio a database that stores the data in shapes, instead of records.

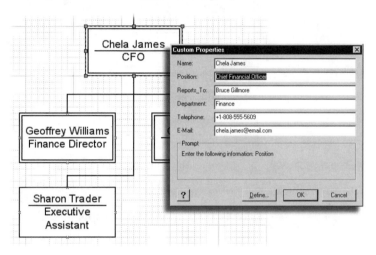

Changes you make to the custom properties are reflected in the diagram:

- Right-click **Chela James** on Page-1.

- From the shortcut menu, select **Properties**. Notice that the Custom Properties dialog box appears, and that the custom property data matches that of the rows in the spreadsheet file, illustrated earlier in the tutorial.

- Change the value of the Position field from "CFO" to "Chief Financial Officer."

- Click **OK**. Notice that Chela James' title has changed.

WARNING: Not all custom property text is linked to the diagram. For example, you might expect that if you change the Reports_To field, Visio would move the shape to its new superior. This, however, does not occur.

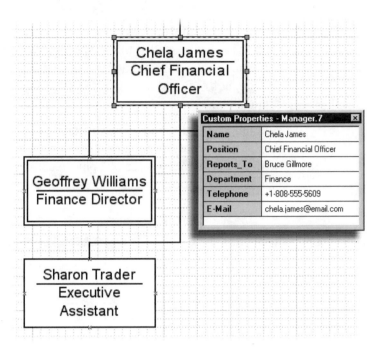

As an alternative, you can open the Custom Properties window. From the menu bar, select **View | Windows | Custom Properties**. Select a shape to view its custom properties. Right-click the Custom Properties window to display a shortcut menu.

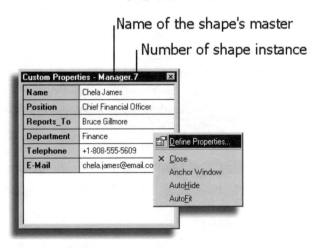

The title bar reads "Custom Properties - Manager.7." "Manager" indicates that this shape is based on the Manager master. "7" means that this is the seventh instance of the Manager master.

Step 11. One of the wonderful aspects of custom properties is that you can easily add data to a shape. Here's how:

- Select the **Chela James** shape.
- Right-click the **Custom Properties** window.
- From the shortcut menu, select **Define Properties**. Notice the Define Custom Properties dialog box.
- Click **New.**
- Enter the following data:
    - Label   **Start Date**
    - Type   **Date**
    - Format   **Long Date**
- Click **OK**.

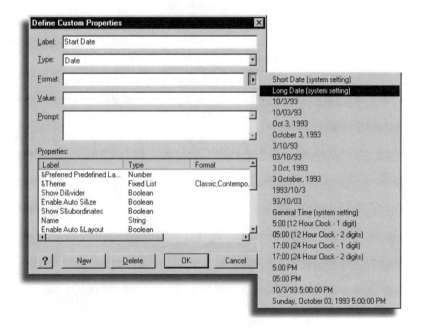

Notice that Start Date is added to the list of custom properties, but that the date value is missing.

Step 12. To add the date, click the **[...]** (date control) button in the Custom Properties window. Notice the calendar. Select a date.

Step 13. The last step of this tutorial is to try out Visio's comparison feature. This lets you see the differences between two otherwise-similar org charts. Follow these steps:

- Make some changes to the org chart by deleting a few shapes: Select a shape, and press the **Delete** key. Notice how Visio 2000 automatically repairs the links between shapes.

- From the menu, select **File | Save As** to save the diagram with a different name: orgchart.vsd.

- From the menu bar, select **Organization Chart | Compare Organization Data**. Notice the Compare Organization Data dialog box.

- Set the following options:
  - My drawing to compare   **orgchart.vsd**
  - Drawing to compare it with   **Ch 6 - Org 2 chart tutorial.vsd**
  - Compare type   **My drawing is newer**

- Click **OK.** Review the changes listed by the Comparison Report dialog box.
- Close the dialog box or save the list as a text file.

Visio Resources

Visio 2000 provides the following resources for creating organization charts. The templates and stencils are found in the \Visio 2000\Solutions\Organization Chart folder.

Related Templates

Organization Chart.Vst

Related Stencils

Organization Chart Shapes.Vss

Related Commands and Wizards

Organization Chart Wizard

This wizard creates an org chart from data stored in the following files:

- Tab- and comma-delimited text (.txt) files
- Org Plus (.txt) files
- Excel (.xls) files
- Microsoft Exchange Server Directory
- Files created by an Open Database Connectivity (ODBC)-compliant database application
- Files generated by enterprise resource planning software, such as PeopleSoft and SAP/R3.

Organization Chart Converter

Visio 2000 uses a new format for org charts. This wizard converts org charts created by earlier versions of Visio. You start this wizard by selecting **Tools | Macros | Organization Chart | Organization Chart Converter.**

Related Toolbars and Menus

The Organization Chart toolbar displays buttons for modifying the look of the organization chart.

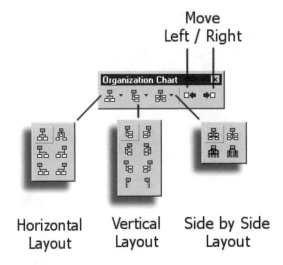

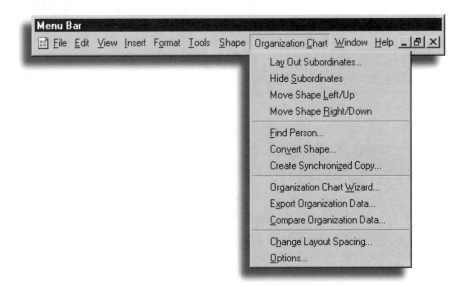

The Organization Chart item is added to the menu bar when you open the Organization Chart solution.

Summary

In this chapter, you learned how to create an organization chart in two ways: by dragging shapes onto the page and by reading data from a file. You found out how to edit the contents of the chart and change the look of the chart. You created a multi-page org chart via synchronization, and learned how to compare the differences between two similar org charts. In addition, you learned about custom properties and how to edit them.

Quiz

1. The easiest way to make one org shape automatically connect to another is to:

   a.   Use the Connect tool.

   b.   Drop one shape on the other.

   c.   Turn on the automatic connect feature.

   d.   Right-click and select Connect.

2. A superior shape is:

   a.   The largest shape on the page.

   b.   The first shape selected.

   c.   A shape above another shape in the reporting structure.

   d.   Any shape on the first page of a multi-page org chart.

3. A subordinate shape is:

   a.   A shape below another shape in the reporting structure.

   b.   The second shape selected.

   c.   The smallest shape on the page.

   d.   Any shape on the second or later page of a multi-page org chart.

4. An org chart can span more than one page.

   True / False

5. The purpose of the Create Synchronized Copy command is:

   a.   Creating a second page in the org chart diagram.

   b.   Ensuring the org chart is up to date.

   c.   The command works only for floor plans.

   d.   There is no such command in Visio 2000.

6. The purpose of the Convert Shape command is:

   a.   Changing the look of all shapes on the page.

   b.   Changing an org shape from one type to another.

   c.   The command works only for flow charts.

   d.   There is no such command in Visio 2000.

7. The purpose of the Correct Shape Copy command is:

   a.   Creating a second page in the org chart diagram.

   b.   Changing the look of all shapes on the page.

   c.   The command works only for directional maps.

Lesson

    d.   There is no such command in Visio 2000.

8. Visio can create an org chart from data stored in files of these formats:

    a.   Ami Pro and WordPerfect.

    b.   PaintShop Pro and PageMaker.

    c.   Navigator and Opera.

    d.   Excel and ASCII.

9. Data in Custom Properties is fixed and cannot be changed.
True / False

10. The Compare feature finds the differences between two org charts.
True / False

Exercises

1. Create a one-page organization chart of your family. Include grandparents, parents, and siblings.

2. Create a two-page, synchronized org chart of your place of work or education.

3. Import the organization data stored in the Sample Org Chart Data.txt file provided with Visio in the \Visio 2000\Samples\Organization Chart folder.

4. Use Visio to re-create the org chart shown in the illustration. You can find a scanned copy of the chart on the companion CD-ROM under the name Ch 6 - Exercise 4.tif.

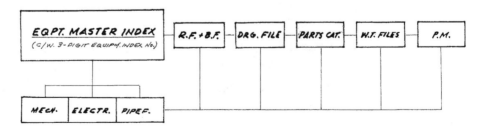

Diagram by Herbert Grabowski

5. Use Visio to re-create the org chart shown in the illustration. You can find a scanned copy of the chart on the companion CD-ROM under the name Ch 6 - Exercise 5.tif.

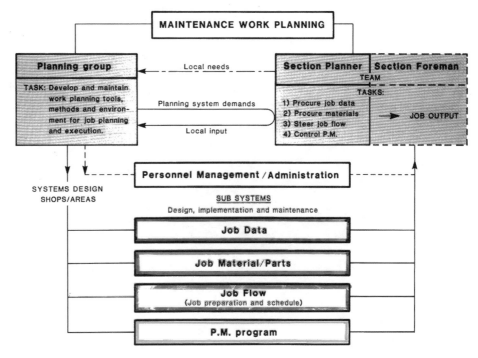

Diagram by Herbert Grabowski

Create a Gantt Chart

What is a Gantt Chart?

The Gantt chart lets you keep track of the phases in a project. In the chart, you specify the tasks required to perform the project, the starting date for each project, and a duration or completion date. Each row in your Gantt chart represents a task. Each task can have a *duration* of minutes, hours, days, or weeks. You can also specify *dependencies* between tasks; this means that one task cannot start (or be completed) until another task starts or finishes. As the project progresses, you update the chart to see how changes in a task affect other tasks and the deadline date.

Tutorials

In the following tutorials, you create a Gantt chart using two different methods. In the basic tutorial, you create the chart within Visio, and in the advanced tutorial, you create the chart data external to Visio. You also learn how to edit the chart and export the chart data to other applications.

Basic: Creating a Gantt Chart

To see how a Gantt chart works, let's work through a tutorial that simulates the stages of creating a catalog. For this tutorial, you use the following data:

Task No.	Catalog Publishing Task	Duration
1	Write product descriptions with Word	1.5 days
2	Take digital photographs	1 week
3	Create database with Access	1 day
4	Typeset catalog with PageMaker	2 days
5	Approve page proofs with Acrobat	2 days
6	Sent files to printer via e-mail	0.5 day
7	Print catalog	2 days
8	Ship to mailing house	1 day

Step 1. Start Visio 2000. In the Welcome to Visio 2000 dialog box, click **OK**.

Step 2. In the Category section of the Choose Drawing Type dialog box, click **Project Schedule**.

Step 3. In the Drawing type box, double-click **Gantt Chart**.

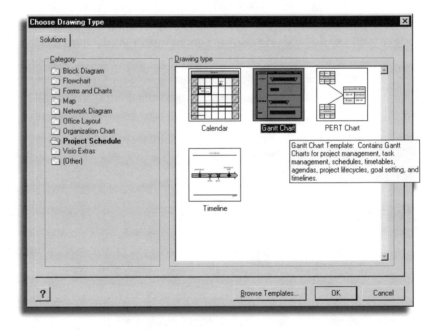

Notice that the Gantt Chart Options dialog box appears.

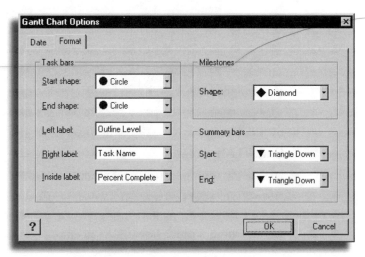

Step 4. In the Date tab, enter the number of tasks and the date-related units. For this tutorial, enter:

- Number of tasks   8
- Duration options Format   **Weeks Days**
- Major units   **Weeks**
- Minor units   **Days**
- Start date   **7 January, 2002**
- End date   **25 January, 2002**

Step 5. Click the **Format** tab. Change the settings to match the following illustration.

TIP: Changing options   The options in the Date and Format tabs are not fixed. You can change them at any time via the **Gantt Chart | Options** command, with the exception of the Number of Tasks (use the **Gantt Chart | Insert Task** command).

Click **OK**. Notice that the Gantt project frame appears on the page, along with the Gantt Chart Shapes stencil. In addition, Visio displays the Gantt Chart toolbar and adds the Gantt Chart item to the menu bar.

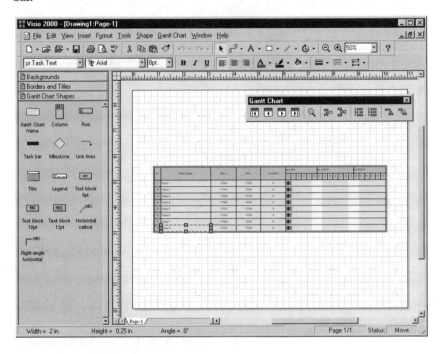

Take a closer look at the Gantt project frame. Notice that it contains several columns:

ID: The sequential number of the task.

Task Name: The name of the task.

Start: The date the task begins.

End: The date the task ends.

Duration: The duration of the task.

Dates: The starting and ending dates you specified earlier in the Gantt Chart Options dialog box. Non-working days (e.g., weekends) are shown in a lighter shade.

The data in each of these columns can be edited, with the exception of ID. To complete the Gantt chart, you need to edit the task names and dates.

ID	Task Name	Start	End	Duration	Jan 6 2002						Jan 13 2002						Jan 20 2002					
					7	8	9	10	11	12	13	14	15	16	17	18	19	20	21	22	23	24	25
1	Task 1	1/7/02	1/7/02	1d																	
2	Task 2	1/7/02	1/7/02	1d																	
3	Task 3	1/7/02	1/7/02	1d																	

Step 6. In the Task Name column, double-click **Task 1**. Replace the text with **Write product descriptions with Word**. Repeat for the remaining task names.

ID	Task Name	Star
1	Write product descriptions with Word	1/7
2	Take digital photographs	1/
3	Create database with Access	1
4	Typeset catalog with PageMaker	1/
5	Approve page proofs with Acrobat	1/7/0
6	Sent files to printer via email	1/7/02
7	Print catalog	1/7/0
8	Ship to mailing house	1/7

Step 7. In the Duration column, double-click **1d**. Replace the text with **1.5d**, which represents one-and-a-half days. Repeat for all durations. Notice that the blue taskbar stretches to match the duration. In addition, the ending date in the End column updates to match the duration.

ID	Task Name	Start	End	Duration	Jan 6 2002		
					7	8	9
1	Write product descriptions with Word	1/7/02	1/8/02	1.50d	0%		
2	Take digital photographs	1/7/02	1/11/02	1w		0%	
3	Create database with Access	1/7/02	1/7/02	1d	0%		
4	Typeset catalog with PageMaker	1/7/02	1/8/02	2d	0%		
5	Approve page proofs with Acrobat	1/7/02	1/8/02	2d	0%		
6	Sent files to printer via email	1/7/02	1/7/02	0.50d	0%		
7	Print catalog	1/7/02	1/8/02	2d	0%		
8	Ship to mailing house	1/7/02	1/7/02	1d	0%		

TIP: Specifying duration   When specifying duration, you may use decimals, such as 1.5, but not fractions. There must be no space between the value and the unit. For example, "2h" is correct, but "2 h" is not. You can specify duration in any format (minutes, hours, days, or weeks), and Visio will convert the units automatically to the default specified in the Gantt Chart Options dialog box. Do not add "s" for plurals. Acceptable duration abbreviations include:

1m = one minute
1h = one hour
1d = one day
1w = one week

Step 8.   Notice that all taskbars have the same start date. In this tutorial, the first two tasks start at the same time, but all other tasks follow each other. Leave taskbars 1 and 2 in place.

- Drag taskbar 3 so that it starts where task 1 ends.
- Repeat for tasks 4 through 7.

Notice that task 5 spans the weekend automatically. Notice, too, that the Start column automatically updates the start dates.

ID	Task Name	Start	End	Duration	Jan 6 2002						Jan 13 2002						Jan 20 2002						
					7	8	9	10	11	12	13	14	15	16	17	18	19	20	21	22	23	24	25
1	Write product descriptions with Word	1/7/02	1/8/02	1.50d	0%																		
2	Take digital photographs	1/7/02	1/11/02	1w		0%																	
3	Create database with Access	1/14/02	1/15/02	1d							1 0%												
4	Typeset catalog with PageMaker	1/15/02	1/17/02	2d								1 0%											
5	Approve page proofs with Acrobat	1/17/02	1/21/02	2d										1 0%									
6	Sent files to printer via email	1/21/02	1/22/02	0.50d													1 0%						
7	Print catalog	1/22/02	1/23/02	2d														1 0%					
8	Ship to mailing house	1/24/02	1/25/02	1d																	1 0%		

Step 9.   With tasks set to their initial positions, the next step is to link tasks. You may have noticed that when you moved a taskbar in Step 8, no other taskbars moved. When *linked*, changing one task affects the other linked tasks. Tasks can be linked by creating *dependencies* or by creating *subtasks*. In this tutorial, you perform both types of linking. First, create dependencies between the taskbars as follows:

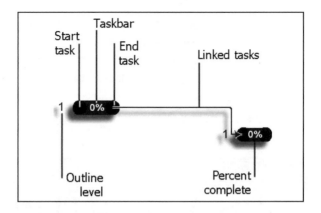

- Select the taskbar belonging to task 2.
- Hold down the **Shift** key, and select the taskbar for task 3.
- From the menu bar, select **Gantt Chart | Link Tasks**. Notice the blue line that connects the two bars.
- Repeat. This time, select all other taskbars (except task 1 and task 2). Right-click, and select **Link Tasks** from the shortcut menu.

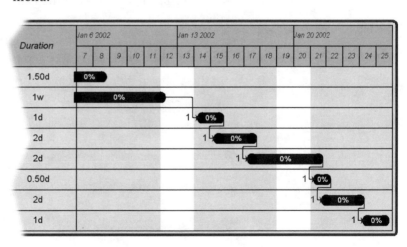

- To see that the tasks bars are truly connected, drag the end of one taskbar longer or shorter. Notice that the linked bars adjust to the new duration.

Step 10. You can break a task into smaller tasks, called *subtasks*. A subtask is linked to its parent task (known as a *summary task*). In this tutorial, task 2 (Take Photographs) is a subtask to 1 (Write Product Descriptions). Create a subtask, as follows:

- Right-click taskbar 2.

- From the shortcut menu, select **Demote Task**. Notice that the parent task displays inverted triangles at the beginning and end of the taskbar. Notice also the text in the Task Name columns; the text of the parent task is in boldface, while the text of the subtask is indented.

- This action links the two tasks. To test this, drag taskbar 1 longer or shorter. Notice how task 2 changes by the same amount.

ID	Task Name	Start	End	Duration	Jan 6 2002					Jan 13 2002						Jan 20 2002					
					7	8	9	10	11	12	13	14	15	16	17	18	19	20	21	22	23	24	25
1	Write product descriptions with Word	1/7/02	1/11/02	1w			0%														
2	Take digital photographs	1/7/02	1/11/02	1w			0%														
3	Create database with Access	1/14/02	1/15/02	1d													1	0%			

Step 11. When we specified the parameters in the Gantt Chart Options dialog box (Step 5), we specified that the taskbars should display the percent complete. So far, the bars show 0% complete. Let's put these into action. To do this, we need to add an extra column. To insert a column:

- Select the Duration column in the chart. Notice the green handles.

- From the menu, select **Gantt Chart | Insert Column**. Notice the Insert Column dialog box.

- From the Column type list, select **Percent Complete**.

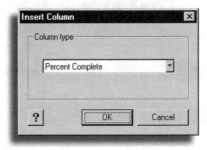

- Click **OK**. Notice that Visio adds the blank column <u>after</u> the column you selected.

- Double-click each 0% text, and replace with values such as 100%, 75%, and 50%. Notice that the percentage is updated on the taskbar. Notice, too, that the percentage complete is shown in pink.

Duration	Percent Complete	Jan 6 2002						Jan 13 2002							Jan 20 2002					
		7	8	9	10	11	12	13	14	15	16	17	18	19	20	21	22	23	24	25
1w	100%				100%															
1w	100%				100%															
1d	100%							100%												
2d	75%								75%											
2d	50%									50%										
0.50d	25%											25%								
2d	0%													0%						
1d	0%															0%				

TIP: Removing columns   To remove a column, select the column, and select **Gantt Chart | Delete Column**. If you made a mistake, you can use the **Edit | Undo** command to return the deleted task.

Step 12.   If necessary, center the Gantt Chart on the page with the **Tools | Center Drawing** command. Save your work by pressing **Ctrl+S**. This drawing can be found on the companion CD-ROM under Ch 7 - Gantt chart tutorial.vsd.

Useful Techniques

To Add and Remove Rows

As your project develops, you may need to add or delete tasks from the chart. To insert or remove a new row (task), select the command from the Gantt Chart menu. To add a task:

- Select a row in the chart. Notice the green handles.
- From the menu, select **Gantt Chart | Insert Task**. Notice that Visio adds the blank row above the row you selected.

As an alternative, you can drag a Row shape from the Gantt Chart Shapes stencil onto the chart; Visio creates a new row where you drop the shape. Another alternative is to drag the project frame taller; Visio 2000 adds new task rows to the chart, keeping the height of each row constant.

To remove a task, select the row, and select **Gantt Chart | Delete Task**. If you made a mistake, you can use the **Edit | Undo** command to return the deleted task.

To Move a Column or Row

You can move any column or row by selecting the column or row and dragging it to its new position. In the case of a row, notice that Visio automatically updates linked data.

To Specify Work Days

By default, Visio assumes that you don't work Saturdays and Sundays, and work from 8:00 A.M. to 4:00 P.M. during the week. You can change these settings, as follows:

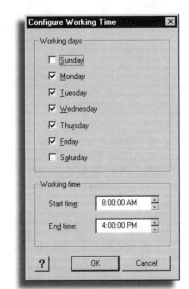

- Right-click the Gantt chart's outline, and select **Configure Working Time**.

- In the dialog box, select the days (and times) that work takes place.

- Click **OK**. Notice that Visio causes the taskbars to bridge over non-work days.

To Change the Connector Type

By default, Visio uses a squared-off S-shape connector to show dependencies. To change to a straight-line connector:

- Right-click the page.

- From the shortcut menu, select **S-type Connectors**.

To View Custom Properties

Each taskbar has a custom property associated with it. To view them, select a taskbar. From the menu bar, select **Shape | Custom Properties**. Notice the Custom Properties dialog box and its many fields. Click **OK** to exit the dialog box.

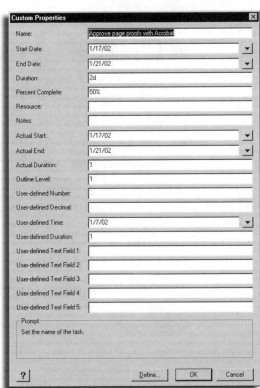

To Print the Chart

The Gantt chart you created in the basic tutorial was designed to fit on a single sheet of paper. More often, however, Gantt charts tend to be too large for a single page. Visio 2000 allows you to *tile* a chart, so that it prints across several pages.

Use the **File | Print Preview** command to ensure the printed result will be what you expect. If necessary, use the **File | Page Setup** command to change the page settings.

Advanced: Importing and Exporting Gantt Chart Data

In the basic tutorial, you created the Gantt chart by entering the data directly in Visio. As an alternative, you can enter the data external to Visio. *External* means using another program other than Visio, such as a spreadsheet, a database, or a text editor. This can be useful when the Gantt data is usually stored external to Visio, and you want to use Visio to visualize the data. Visio can read properly formatted Gantt data stored in the following file types:

File Extension	Meaning
CSV	Comma-delimited text
MPX	Microsoft Project Exchange
TXT	Tab-delimited text
XLS	Microsoft Excel

Visio provides a pair of templates in the \Visio 2000\Solutions\Project Schedule folder called Gantt Data Template.txt for creating files in comma-delimited format, and Gantt Data Template.xlt for creating a files in Excel (.xls) format. Both files contain the header, as shown below:

```
Task #,Task Name,Duration,Start Date,End Date,Dependency,Resource
```

Visio uses a program called Import Project Data.exe to import data by two methods:

- Read the data stored in an MPX, CSV, TXT, or XLS file.
- Create the data, which will be stored (then read) in a text or Excel file.

In this advanced tutorial, we will work through the second method: create the data, then read it.

Step 1.   Continue with Visio open from the basic tutorial. (If necessary, double-click the Ch 7 - Gantt chart tutorial.vsd file to start Visio with the Gantt diagram.) Press **Ctrl+N** to start a new, blank drawing.

Step 2.　When the Gantt Chart Options dialog box appears, click **Cancel**.

Step 3.　From the menu bar, select **Gantt Chart | Create Data File | Microsoft Excel Workbook**. (If you do not have Excel installed on your computer, you can use **Gantt Chart | Create Data File | Text File** instead. The steps are very similar, but Excel is easier for creating the Gantt data.) Notice the Import Project Data dialog box.

Step 4.　Click **OK**. Notice that Excel opens, and displays the Gantt Data Template1 spreadsheet. Notice also that row 1 contains header text, which helps you enter the correct data.

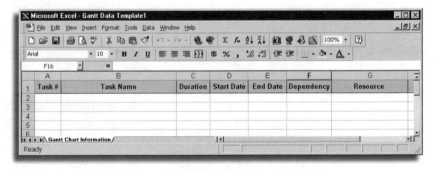

Step 5.　In row 2, enter the following data:

- Task #　　　　　**1**
- Task Name　　　**Write product descriptions with Word**
- Duration　　　　**1.5 days**
- Start Date　　　**7 Jan 2002**
- End Date　　　　It is not necessary to enter any data here, since Visio will work it out based on the duration and start date.

	Dependency	Leave blank
■	Resource	Leave blank. Optionally, you can enter any data here, such as a description of the resources required. This data is displayed by the Gantt chart if the Resource column is added.

Step 6. Enter the remaining data, as illustrated in the following table:

Task #	Task Name	Duration	Start Date	End Date	Dependency	Resource
2	Take digital photographs	1 week	7 Jan 2002			
3	Create database with Access	1 day	14 Jan 2002		2	
4	Typeset catalog with PageMaker	2 days	15 Jan 2002		3	
5	Approve page proofs with Acrobat	2 days	17 Jan 2002		4	
6	Sent files to printer via email	0.5 day	21 Jan 2002		5	
7	Print catalog	2 days	22 Jan 2002		6	
8	Ship to mailing house	1 day	24 Jan 2002		7	

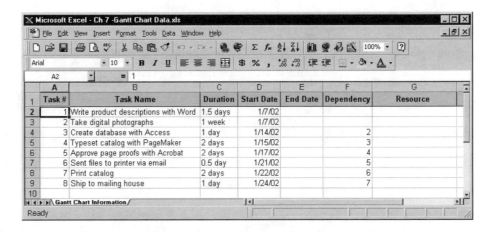

Step 7. Save the file using the **Ctrl+S** shortcut. The spreadsheet file can be found on the companion CD-ROM under the name Ch 7 - Gantt Chart Data.xls.

Step 8.   Return to Visio. From the menu bar, select **Gantt Chart | Import**. Notice that the Import Project Data dialog box looks different from Step 3.

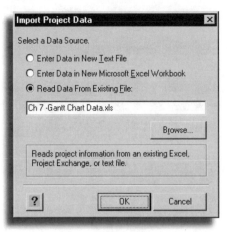

TIP: Macros in Excel   The Excel template includes three macros, which you can access via **Tools | Macro | Macros**. While the use of macros in Microsoft Office applications can leave your computer vulnerable to dangerous data-destroying viruses, expert users may want to employ these macros: Auto_Open, Auto_Close, and RunImportProjectData.

Step 9.   Select the **Read Data From Existing File** option. Click the **Browse** button, select the .xls file you saved earlier, and click **Open**. Click **OK**. Notice the Gantt Chart Options dialog box, which should be familiar from the basic tutorial.

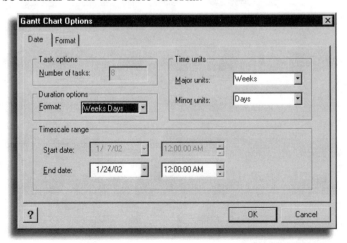

Step 10. Make the following changes to the Gantt Chart Options dialog box:

- Duration options Format   **Weeks Days**
- Major units   **Weeks**
- Minor units   **Days**

Click **OK**. Wait a minute or two while Visio generates the chart.

ID	Task Name	Start	End	Duration	Jan 6 2002						Jan 13 2002						Jan 20 2002				
					7	8	9	10	11	12	13	14	15	16	17	18	19	20	21	22	23	24
1	Write product descriptions with Word	1/7/02	1/8/02	1.50d																		
2	Take digital photographs	1/7/02	1/11/02	1w																		
3	Create database with Access	1/14/02	1/14/02	1d																		
4	Typeset catalog with PageMaker	1/15/02	1/16/02	2d																		
5	Approve page proofs with Acrobat	1/17/02	1/18/02	2d																		
6	Sent files to printer via email	1/21/02	1/21/02	0.50d																		
7	Print catalog	1/22/02	1/23/02	2d																		
8	Ship to mailing house	1/24/02	1/24/02	1d																		

Step 11. You can export the data from the Gantt chart as an MPX file, which is read by Microsoft Project Exchange and some other programs:

- From the menu bar, select **Gantt Chart | Export**. Notice the Save As dialog box.
- Select the folder in which to save the file. If necessary, you can change the filename.
- Click **Save**.

You can now open the MPX file in another application.

Visio Resources

Visio 2000 provides the following resources for creating Gantt charts. The template, stencil, and files are found in the \Visio 2000\Solutions\Project Schedule folder:

Related Templates

Gantt Chart.Vst

Related Stencils

Gantt Chart Shapes.Vss

Related Commands and Wizards

Gantt Chart Wizard

This wizard creates a Gantt chart from scratch. It prompts you for the basic parameters, such as number of tasks, and project start and end dates. The wizard then draws the basic Gantt chart, which you can edit. You start this wizard by selecting Tools | Macros | Project Schedule | Gantt Chart Wizard.

Import Project Data

This application imports data from TXT and XLS files to create a Gantt chart. There are several ways to start this program. Outside of Visio, double-click Import Project Data.Exe found in the \Visio 2000\Solutions\Project Schedule folder. Inside of Visio, select **Tools | Macros | Project Schedule | Import Project Data**, or select **Gantt Chart | Create Data File**.

Related Toolbars and Menus

The Gantt Chart toolbar displays buttons for modifying the look of the organization chart.

The Gantt Chart item is added to the menu bar when you open the Gantt Chart solution.

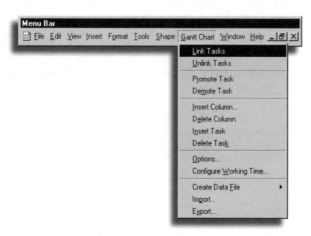

Related Files

The following files contain the header for creating a Gantt data file using Note-pad (for plain ASCII data) or Excel 5.0/97 or later (for spreadsheet data). Although Visio uses these files for its Import Project Data routine, you can use these files for your own manual data input:

- Gantt Data Template.Txt
- Gantt Data Template.Xls

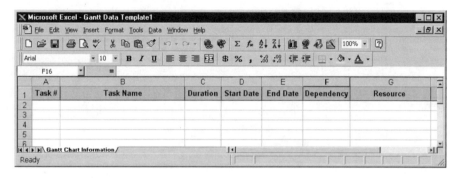

Summary

In this chapter, you learned how to create a Gantt chart using two methods: by entering data directly in Visio and by reading data from an external source. You also learned how to edit the chart by adding, moving, and removing rows and columns.

Quiz

1. What is the purpose of a Gantt chart?
   a. Illustrates the grants given to charitable agencies.
   b. Shows the relationship between departments in a large national government.
   c. Keeps track of the phases of a project.
   d. Kept track of the progress in the American Civil War.

2. Which one of the following is <u>not</u> a duration?
   a. Days
   b. Bytes
   c. Hours
   d. Weeks

3. A dependent task cannot start until another task starts.
   True / False

4. For each task, Visio requires the start date, duration, and the end date.
   True / False

5. The data in all columns can be edited, with one exception. Which column cannot be edited?

   a.   ID

   b.   Task Name

   c.   Start

   d.   Duration

6. Match the abbreviation with its meaning:

   a.   m   i.   day

   b.   d   ii.   week

   c.   h   iii.   minute

   d.   w   iv.   hour

7. Match the abbreviation with its meaning:

   a.   CSV   i.   Microsoft Project Exchange

   b.   MPX   ii.   Microsoft Excel

   c.   TXT   iii.   Comma-delimited text

   d.   XLS   iv.   Tab-delimited text

8. Visio can create a Gantt chart based on:

   a.   Data entered within Visio.

   b.   Data entered in a software program external to Visio.

   c.   Both of the above.

   d.   None of the above.

9. Large Gantt charts can be printed across more than one page.
   True / False

10. The Gantt Chart Wizard imports data from external sources.
    True / False

Exercises

1. Open the Ch 7 - Gantt chart tutorial.vsd diagram on the companion CD-ROM. Add two more tasks:

Task No.	Catalog Publishing Task	Duration
9	Export catalog to Web site	2.5 days
10	Send out email marketing message	0.5 days

2. Open the Ch 7 - Gantt chart tutorial.vsd diagram on the companion CD-ROM. Add two more columns next to duration: Actual Start Date and Actual End Date. Populate the columns with appropriate dates.

3. Print out the Gantt chart you created in exercise #2 large enough to cover two sheets of paper.

4. Create a Gantt chart for the construction of a house. Employ at least six tasks.

5. Create a Gantt chart for the construction of a space station. Employ at least 12 tasks.

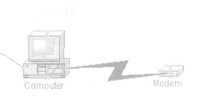

Create a Network Diagram

In this chapter, you learn about:

♦ Creating a network diagram

♦ Adding custom properties to shapes

♦ Collecting data and creating a report within Visio

♦ Exporting data to an external file

♦ Additional methods of creating network diagrams via Visio Network Equipment, Visio 2000 Professional Edition, and Visio 2000 Enterprise Edition

What is a Network Diagram?

A *network diagram* illustrates your computer network. Its purpose is to show the location and connection of all computers, hubs, and peripherals on the network. The network can be a LAN (local area network, within one building) or a WAN (wide area network, spans several buildings). Because network wiring is usually hidden behind desks and inside ceilings, it is useful to document how computers are connected.

The network diagramming features in Visio 2000 Standard and Technical editions are strictly manual. You drag masters from the network shape stencils onto the page and you manually draw (using connectors) the network wires between devices. The more advanced versions of Visio, Professional and Enterprise editions, have methods to automatically document networks.

You can include data (called custom properties) with each shape in the network diagram. This lets you keep track of information, such as asset numbers and device descriptions. Visio includes a couple of methods for creating reports from that data.

Tutorials

In the following tutorials, you create a network diagram, then produce a report listing all the equipment.

Basic: Making a Network Diagram

In this basic tutorial, you quickly create a network diagram by dragging masters from the stencil onto the page.

Step 1. Start Visio. When the Welcome to Visio 2000 dialog box appears, double-click the **Choose drawing type** option.

Step 2. In the Category section of the Choose Drawing Type dialog box, click **Network Diagram**, and then double-click the **Basic Network** option.

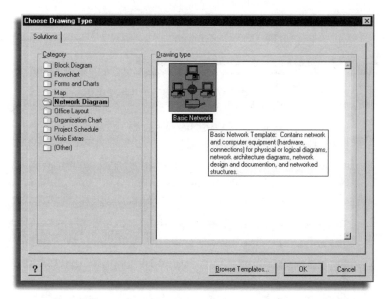

Step 3. Notice that Visio opens a new blank drawing. At the left are three stencils that hold the SmartShapes symbols: Basic Network Shapes, Basic Network Shapes 2, and Basic Network Shapes 3D. The page is oriented horizontally (wider than tall).

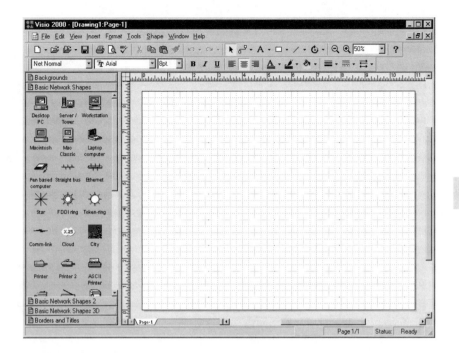

Step 4.   To make the diagram look more interesting, let's use the "three-dimensional" shapes. Click the title bar of the **Basic Network Shapes 3D** stencil. (The shapes aren't actually 3-D; it would be more accurate to call them isometric, which simulates a 3-D look.)

Step 5.   Drag several masters onto the page. For example, place the **Hub** shape in the center of the page. Place a **Server** shape below the hub. Place five **Personal computer** shapes around the hub. Add the **Printer** shape below the server. Place the **Modem** shape near one of the personal computers.

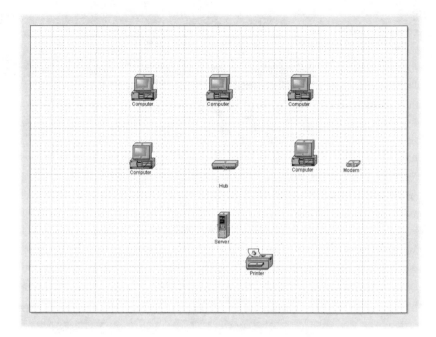

TIP: Layer segregation   Visio places the network shapes on appropriate layers. For example, products manufactured by IBM are placed on the "IBM" layer. The Network Diagram solution creates five layers automatically: Apple, Cray, Digital, IBM, and Network. The Network layer is for all shapes that don't belong in the other four layers. To view the layers, select **View | Layer Properties** from the menu bar.

Step 6.   Let's connect the network together. We'll use the Line-curve connector, which you find in the Basic Network Shapes stencil. Click the title bar of the **Basic Network Shapes** stencil. Scroll down the stencil to find the Line-curve connector.

Step 7.   Drag the **Line-curve connector** to one of the personal computer shapes. Move the connector until you see a red square on the computer ①. This indicates the connector is *glued* to the computer, which means that the connector moves with the computer when you move the computer. Drag the free end of the connector toward the hub ②. Let go of the mouse button when you see the red square on the hub shape ③.

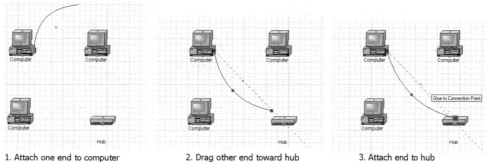

1. Attach one end to computer   2. Drag other end toward hub   3. Attach end to hub

To see the effect of glue, drag the personal computer shape anywhere on the page. Notice how the connector follows along. Press **Ctrl+Z** to undo the move, putting the shape back in its original position.

Step 8. Connect all personal computer shapes and the server shape to the hub. Connect the printer to the server. Attach the Comm-link shape to the modem.

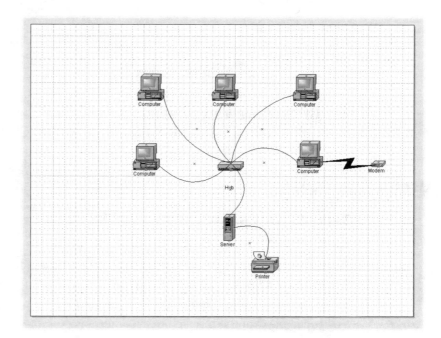

Step 9. The final step is to dress up the diagram. From the Backgrounds stencil, drag the **Background high-tech** master onto the page. Click **Yes** when Visio asks, "Do you want this shape to be the background image for this page?"

From the Borders and Titles stencil, drag the **Border technical 2** onto the page. If necessary, move the border into a position that doesn't interfere with the diagram. If you wish, fill in the border's information, such as name and date.

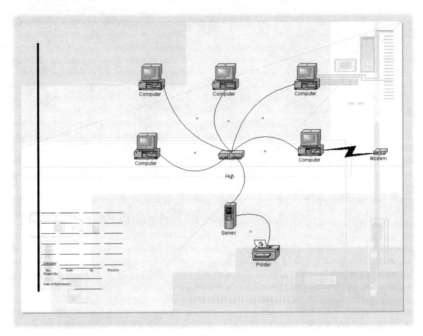

Step 10. Save your work by pressing **Ctrl+S**. This diagram can be found on the companion CD-ROM under the name of Ch 8 - Network diagram tutorial.vsd.

Useful Techniques

Get a Quick Count

As noted in the basic tutorial, Visio stores shapes on appropriate layers. The Layer Properties dialog box contains a column that counts the number of shapes on each layer. This can be a quick way of counting items in the diagram:

■ From the menu bar, select **View | Layer Properties**. Notice the Layer Properties dialog box.

■ In the header row, click the **#** button. This forces Visio to count all shapes on each layer.

■ Click **OK** to dismiss the dialog box.

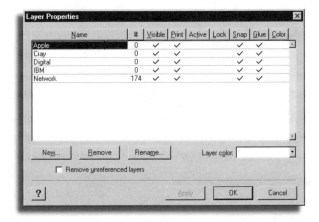

Number the Devices

You can have Visio number network devices in the order that you specify. Here's how:

- From the menu bar, select **Tools | Macros | Visio Extras | Number Shapes**. Notice the Number Shapes dialog box.

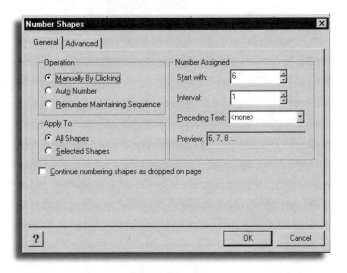

- In the Number Shapes dialog box, specify options. Options you may want to consider include Start with number, Interval, and Preceding Text. Ensure that the manual numbering option is selected.

- Click **OK**. Notice the Manual Numbering dialog box.

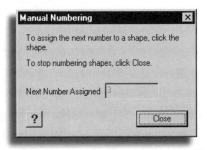

- Click on shapes in the order you want them numbered. Notice that Visio places the number above the text in each shape.
- When done, click the **Close** button on the Manual Numbering dialog box.

Advanced Numbering Options

Click the Advanced tab of the Number Shapes dialog box to see additional options, such as where the number is placed, and whether the number should be hidden.

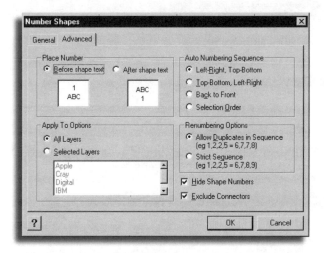

Advanced: Producing a Network Equipment Report

In this advanced tutorial, you produce a report of the network equipment in the diagram.

Step 1. Ensure Visio is still open from the basic tutorial. If necessary, open the Ch 8 - Network diagram tutorial.vsd file from the companion CD-ROM.

Step 2. Let's add some data to the shapes. Here's how:
- Right-click a shape. Notice the shortcut menu ①.
- From the shortcut menu, select **Properties**. Notice the Custom Properties dialog box ②.

1.

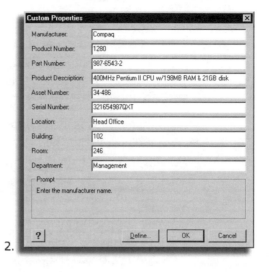

2.

- Fill in the data for as many of the fields as you want. For example:
  - Manufacturer **Compaq**
  - Product Number **1280**
  - Part Number **987-6543-2**
  - Product Description **400MHz Pentium II CPU w/198MB RAM & 21GB disk**
  - Asset Number **34-486**
  - Serial Number **321654987QXT**
  - Location **Head Office**
  - Building **102**
  - Room **246**
  - Department **Management**

  Click **OK**. The data you entered is stored with the shape. Later in this tutorial, we extract the data into a report.

  Step 3. Repeat the process for the remaining shapes in the diagram. Enter as much data as you feel like in the Custom Properties dialog box for each computer and peripheral. When done, press **Ctrl+S** to save your work.

  If you find it tedious entering so much data, open Ch 8 - Network report tutorial.vsd found on the companion CD-ROM. This diagram has custom properties entered for all shapes on the page.

Step 4.   Let's extract the data about this network into a report. Visio provides a couple of ways of doing this; one method creates a report within Visio, the other method exports the data to a file outside of Visio. We work through both methods.

The more general method is via the Tools | Property Report command. This is available for all types of Visio diagrams. You can create a report within Visio, as follows:

- Create a new page for the report. Right-click the **Page-1** tab, and select **Insert Page**. Specify a new foreground page named "Report." Click **OK** to exit the Page Setup dialog box.

- From the menu, select **Tools | Property Report**. Notice the Property Reporting Wizard.

- Click **Next**. Specify the following options:

  - Range   **Document**
  - Include   **All shapes with custom property: Asset Number.**

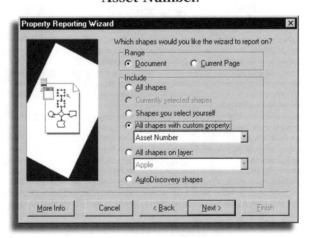

- Click **Next**. In the Numeric area, select **Total**.

TIP: Numeric options   When you select one of the Numeric options—Total, Average, Median, Minimum, or Maximum—Visio includes the formula as the last line in the spreadsheet. For example, the Average option causes Visio to include =ROUND(AVERAGE(D1:D17),0) on the last line.

When you select **Custom**, Visio adds no formula to the last line. You will need to enter your own formula in the spreadsheet cells.

Select **Basic Inventory** to create an inventory report. A bug in this wizard causes Visio to report only the property you selected earlier (such as Asset Number). The Total identical items option groups duplicate shapes.

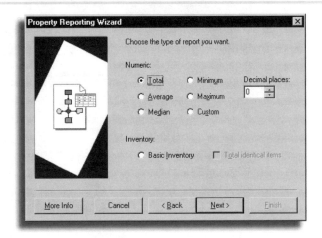

- Click **Next**. Wait a minute or two while Visio generates the report. Notice the summary page, which looks like a spreadsheet. Examine the data that Visio collected. You can, if you wish, click **Back** to change the data generated by the report.

Notice the **Save** button with the diskette icon. Click the icon to save the data to a file. You have the option of saving in Tabbed Text or Microsoft Excel 5.0 format. If you wish, save the data under the name "Network Report.xls." A copy of this file is available on the companion CD-ROM.

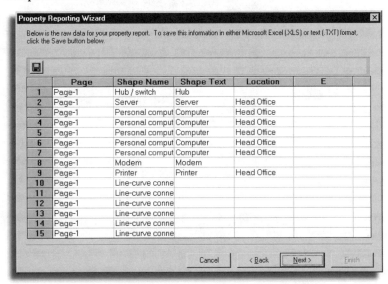

- Click **Next**. Here you can customize the header for the report. To edit a label, click the name under Label and type the new label.

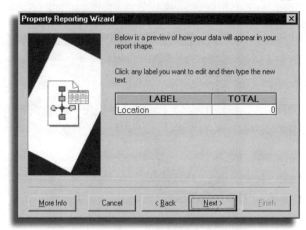

- Click **Next**. Here you specify more parameters of the report. Make the following changes:

  - Type a title   **Network Report**
  - Choose the drawing page   **Report**
  - Display column headings   ✓

The Include sub-total reports option creates a report on every page of the diagram.

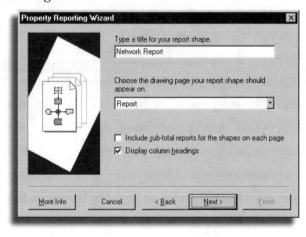

- Click **Next**. Here you specify more options. You might as well turn on all options.

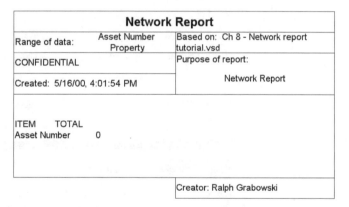

- Click **Finish**. Notice that Visio spends a few minutes creating the report. I have found that this wizard does a poor job collecting data. You may find—as I have all through Visio versions 4, 5, and 2000—that nothing is reported.

Network Report		
Range of data: Asset Number Property		Based on: Ch 8 - Network report tutorial.vsd
CONFIDENTIAL		Purpose of report:
Created: 5/16/00, 4:01:54 PM		Network Report
ITEM TOTAL Asset Number 0		
		Creator: Ralph Grabowski

Step 5. The alternative method of creating a report is specific to network diagrams. Unlike the Property Reporting Wizard, this method works correctly. Tools | Export Network Inventory creates an external report in plain text, Excel (spreadsheet), and Access (database) formats.

- From the menu bar, select **Tools | Export Network Inventory**. Notice the Export Network Inventory dialog box.

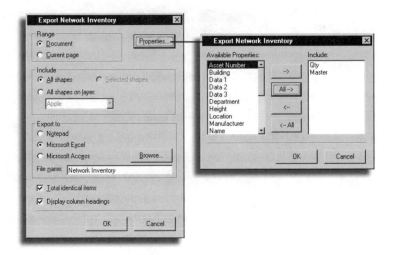

- Click **Properties**. Notice the second dialog box.
- Click **All ->**. Notice that all properties move over to the Include column.
- Click **OK** to exit the secondary dialog box.
- Back in the main dialog box, ensure the following options are set:
  - Range   **Document**
  - Include   **All shapes**
  - Export to   **Microsoft Excel**
  - File name   **Network Inventory**
  - Total identical items   ✓
  - Display column headings   ✓
- Click **OK**, and wait a minute or two as Visio exports the data. Notice that Visio automatically launches Excel, which displays the data. The data includes superfluous items, such as the background and border shapes, which I have deleted from the spreadsheet shown in the illustration.

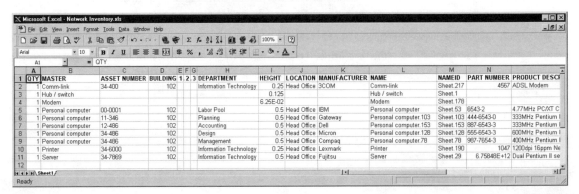

You may exit Excel and Visio with **Alt+F4**.

Visio Resources

Visio 2000 provides the following resources for creating network diagrams. The templates and stencils are found in the \Visio 2000\Solutions\Network Diagram folder.

Related Templates

Basic Network.Vst

Related Stencils

Basic Network Shapes.Vss
Basic Network Shapes 2.Vss
Basic Network Shapes 3D.Vss

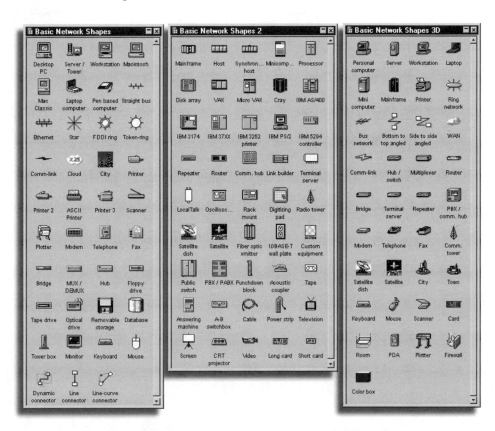

Related Commands

Tools | Export Network Inventory

Creates a report of all network equipment in three formats: plain ASCII, Excel spreadsheet, and Access database.

Additional Resources

The Standard and Technical editions of Visio 2000 provide just rudimentary support for network diagramming. If you need to work a lot with networks, consider these products from Microsoft: Visio Network Equipment, Visio 2000 Professional Edition, and Visio 2000 Enterprise Edition.

Visio Network Equipment is an add-on that provides tens of thousands of vendor-specific network equipment shapes. These shapes are much more detailed than those provided in the Basic Network Shapes stencils. Most shapes include custom properties in four categories: asset, equipment, maintenance, and network. Through a subscription plan, you receive additional shapes three times a year.

Visio 2000 Professional Edition (http://www.visio.com/visio2000/professional/) adds the following features to those found in Standard Edition:

- Network design and documentation
- Directory services diagramming for Active Directory, LDAP, and Novell
- Database design and reengineering of most client/server databases, desktop databases, and Microsoft Repository
- Software diagramming and code generation, including the reverse engineering of Visual Studio project, and support for UML v1.2
- Advanced data flow diagramming
- Web site mapping

Visio 2000 Enterprise Edition (http://www.visio.com/visio2000/enterprise/) includes all the features found in Professional Edition, plus these:

- Visio Network Equipment
- Automatic documentation of the network using SNMP on WAN, LAN, Layer 3 (IP network), and Layer 2 (data link)
- Import of data directly from a directory service database; export in LDIF format
- Collaborative database design
- Business rules-based database design via Object Role Modeling
- Generation of UML code

Summary

In this chapter, you learned how to create a network diagram. You also learned how to add custom properties to shapes, then create a report from that data.

Quiz

1. Visio 2000 Standard Edition can automatically create a network diagram.
   True / False

2. The 3-D network shapes included with Visio are actually isometric.
   True / False

3. Visio places vendor-specific network shapes on separate layers.
   True / False

4. When attaching a connector to a shape, the red square means:
   a. The connector cannot attach to the shape.
   b. The connector is glued to the shape.
   c. The wrong connector is being used.
   d. The shape is glued to the connector.

5. When a connector and a shape are glued together, this means:
   a. Neither the shape nor the connector can move.
   b. Moving the connector drags the shape with it.
   c. Moving the shape drags the connector with it.
   d. The shape moves, but the connector stays in place.

6. To undo the most recent action, press the following keystrokes:
   a. Ctrl+U
   b. Alt+U
   c. Alt+Z
   d. Ctrl+Z

7. The Layer Properties dialog box displays the number of shapes on each page.
   True / False

8. Visio can number shapes automatically in the order that you pick the shapes.
   True / False

9. Only specific shapes can contain custom properties.

   True / False

10. The Export Network Inventory command creates a report of network equipment.

    True / False

Exercises

1. Open the Ch 8 - Network diagram tutorial.vsd file found on the companion CD-ROM. Connect three more computers and another printer to the network.

2. Continuing with the diagram you created in exercise #1, use the Tools | Export Network Inventory command to create a report. Export the report in plain ASCII, XLS, or database format. Open the file in Notebook, Excel, or Access to view the result. Print the report.

3. Create a network diagram from scratch. You can use your imagination, or copy the network located at your place of study or work. Include at least one hub, one server, one printer, and four computers. Remember that all devices (computers and printers) must connect back to the hub. Save your work, and print it out.

4. Re-create the coax (10Base-2) network shown in the following illustration. The image is available on the companion CD-ROM under the name Ch 8 - Exercise 4.tif.

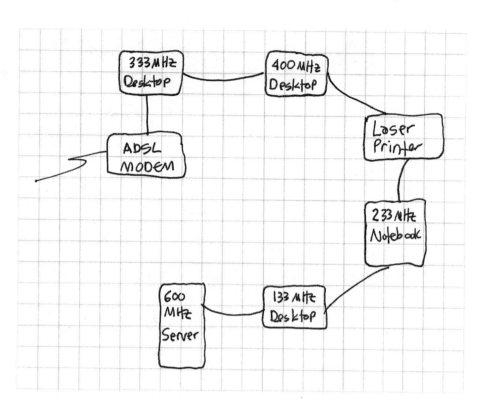

5. Re-create the twisted pair (10Base-T) network shown in the following illustration. The image is available on the companion CD-ROM under the name Ch 8 - Exercise 5.tif.

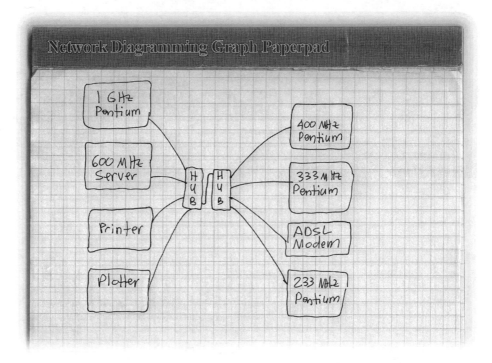

Create an Office Layout

What is an Office Layout?

Office layouts are also known as floor plans or space plans. Floor plans typically show the walls, door, and windows that define the boundaries of the rooms. Inside each room, the furniture is located—desks, chairs, plants, computers, and other office equipment.

Floor plans are typically drawn to scale so that everything is placed in accurate relation to each other. As an option, Visio allows you to include dimensions, which show distances and lengths. For example, dimensions are commonly used to show the length of a wall, the width of a door, and the clearance between a desk and another object.

Creating an office layout is useful for keeping track of office furniture inventory. You may want to create a layout of your office, as it is presently arranged, in preparation for a move or remodeling. If you wish, you can place different layouts on layers; turning layers on and off allows you to instantly see the changes.

Tutorials

In the following tutorials, you create a floor plan of an office, then export the floor plan to a Web page.

In this chapter, you learn about:

♦ Creating a floor plan with walls, doors, windows, and furniture

♦ The importance of scale and the elements of a dimension

♦ Adding Internet hyperlinks to the furniture

♦ Exporting the floor plan as a Web page

♦ Viewing the Web page in GIF and VML formats.

Basic: Making a Floor Plan

In this basic tutorial, you create the floor plan of an office.

Step 1. Start Visio. When the Welcome to Visio 2000 dialog box appears, double-click the **Choose drawing type** option.

Step 2. In the Category section of the Choose Drawing Type dialog box, click **Office Layout**, and then double-click the **Office Layout** option.

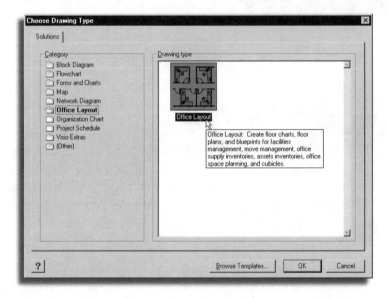

Step 3. Notice that Visio opens a new blank drawing. At the left is a stencil that holds the SmartShapes symbols: Office Layout Shapes. The page is in landscape orientation (horizontal is wider than vertical).

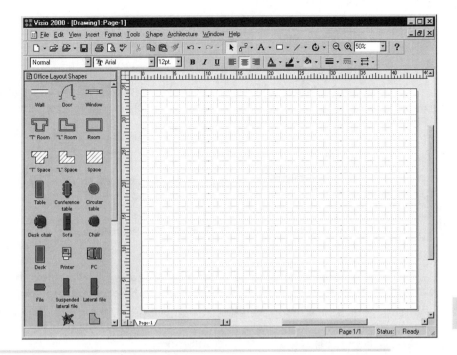

TIP: Scaling floor plans   Floor plan drawings are always drawn *to scale*. The reason is easy: A room is larger than a sheet of paper. So, the room has to be drawn small enough to fit the paper. By default, Visio uses a scale of ¼" = 1', which means that every quarter-inch on the page is the same as one foot in the room. (My children are taught only the metric system in school. For them, the scale works out to 1:48—1cm on the page equals 48cm in the room.)

At the default scale of ¼" = 1', the typical 11" x 8½" sheet of paper is large enough for a floor area of 42' x 32'. If this is not large enough for your project, you can change the scale, as follows:

- From the menu bar, select **File | Page Setup**. Notice the Page Setup dialog box.

- Click the **Drawing Scale** tab. Notice the Drawing scale area on the left.

- Under Predefined scale, select a smaller scale.

- Click **OK**.

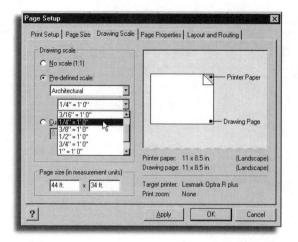

A smaller scale would be one like 3/16" = 1', which lets the paper handle an area of 56' x 42'. This scale would be good for drawing the floor plan of an entire house. Alternatively, if the page represents too large an area, select a larger scale, such as 1" = 1' (represents a floor area of 10.5' x 8', which is sufficient for a small room).

Here is how to calculate scale numbers:

1. Convert to common units:
   ¼" = 1' becomes ¼" = 12" (there are 12" in 1')

2. Convert unit scale:
   ¼" = 12" becomes 1" = 48" (here, both sides are multiplied by 4)

3. Multiple the page's size by the unit scale. Since most printers cannot print on the full page, reduce the page size by ¼" on all four sides. This space is called the *margin*. For example, the typical 11" x 8.5" sheet becomes 10.5" x 8".
   10.5" x 8" becomes 504" x 384" (multiply by 48).

4. Reduce to feet:
   504" x 384" becomes 42' x 32' (divide both sides by 12").

Step 4. Drag the **Space** master ① onto the page. Notice that Visio creates a square room with an area of 100 square feet ②.

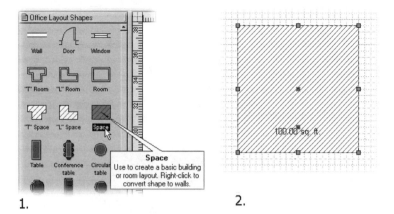

1.   2.

Step 5. Let's make the room bigger. Drag the right handle to the right ①, keeping an eye on the status line Stop when the status line reads Width = 20 ft. ②. Notice that the square footage updates itself automatically: 200 sq. ft.

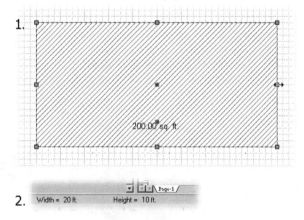

Step 6. Repeat, this time making the space taller. Drag the lower handle downward until the status line reads Height = 15 ft. The area of the room is now 300 sq. ft.

TIP: Relocating text   Notice the two handles (small green squares) inside the space. One handle is directly above the 300 sq. ft. You can drag this handle to relocate the text.

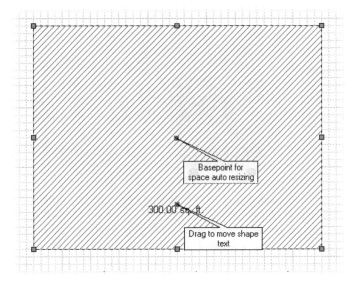

The second handle is in the center of the space. You drag this handle to specify the location of the basepoint for space resizing.

Step 7.   With the room sized, let's convert the space into walls. Right-click the space. From the shortcut menu, select **Convert to Walls** ①. Notice the Convert to Walls dialog box ②.

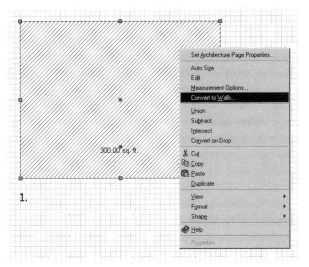

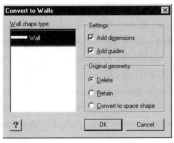

The Convert to Walls dialog box has the following options:

Wall shape type: Lists wall shapes from all open stencils. In most cases, just one wall type appears.

Add dimensions: Adds dimensions to the walls.

Add guides: Add guidelines to the walls.

Delete original geometry: Erases the original space shape after walls are drawn.

Retain original geometry: Keeps the original space shape after conversion.

Convert to space shape: Converts walls back to the space shape.

Wall endpoints and dimension endpoints will be glued to the intersection of wall guides. You can drag guides to resize spaces that you create. Be sure to select this box if you plan on resizing spaces.

Step 8. Ensure all options are set as shown in the illustration, and click **OK**. Notice that Visio converts the space into four walls, complete with dimensions. The walls are pairs of parallel lines, with white fill. The guidelines allow you to stretch the space larger and smaller; Visio updates the dimensions automatically.

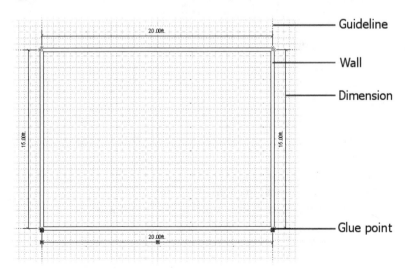

TIP: Dimensions   A *dimension* indicates distances, lengths, and angles. A dimension consists of four parts:

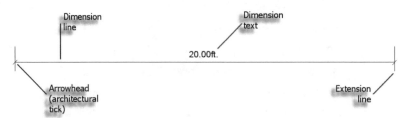

Dimension line: Indicates the length being measured.
Dimension text: Describes the measurement, such as 20.00 ft.
Extension lines: Point to the two ends being measured.
Arrowheads: Can be literal arrowheads (← and →) or symbols specific to a discipline. The illustration shows tick marks commonly used by architects.

Notice that the dimension has four green handles. These allow you to change Visio dimensions:

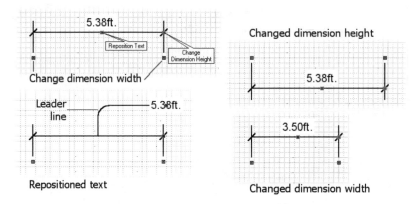

Change dimension width: Drag either of the two handles under the extension line. These position the dimension relative to the object being measured.
Change dimension height: Drag the handle to make the extension lines longer and shorter; also mirrors the dimension.
Reposition text: Drag the handle to relocate the dimension text. When the text gets too far away from its dimension, Visio adds the leader line automatically.

Step 9.   Let's add a door and some windows. Drag the **Door** master onto the page. Locate the door on the lower wall. Let go of the mouse button when Visio reports "Glue to guide."

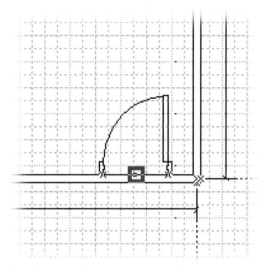

Drag several **Window** masters onto the page. Locate windows on all four walls. Notice that the window rotates into place. The Window shape has a single handle (called "Set Width"), which allows you to drag the window wider or narrower. Try changing the size of some windows.

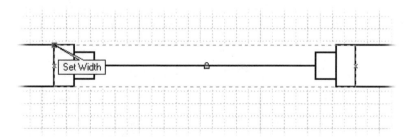

Your diagram should look similar to the following illustration.

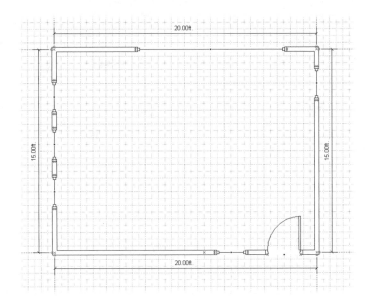

TIP: Accurate sizes   While the design of Visio encourages you to drag shapes, this is not the most accurate way to draw. Floor plans, in particular, must usually be accurate to the nearest 1" or ¼". To accurately size the walls, doors, and windows, right-click them and select Set Properties, as follows:

Doors: Set Door Properties
Walls: Set Wall Properties
Windows: Set Window Properties

The Set Properties dialog boxes allow you to specify the width, height, and other sizes accurately. There are many options available, as shown by the window example in the illustration.

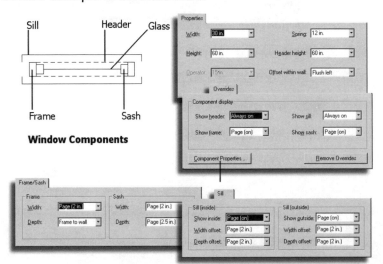

Window Components

Step 10. Let's populate the room with some furniture. Drag the **Conference table** master into the room. Also drag the **Circular table** master, and place it in the corner. Surround the round table with a couple of **Chair** shapes. Place the **Plant** shape on top of the round table. Your diagram should look something like the following illustration.

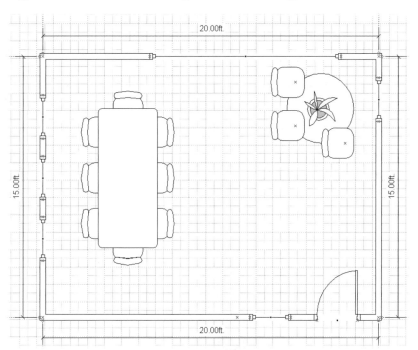

TIP: Relocating the ruler zero

The zero location for the two rulers is usually the lower-left corner of the page. To help you position furniture, doors, and windows relative to a corner of the room, you can relocate the zero point of the rulers. Hold down the Ctrl key, then drag the cursor from the ruler onto the page, such as the lower-left corner of the room. When you let go of the mouse button, notice that the ruler's zero has been relocated.

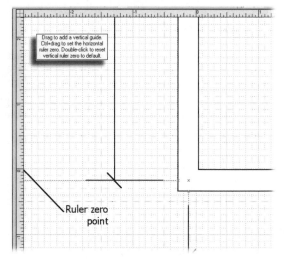

To return the rulers' zero to their original position, double-click each ruler.

Step 11. Notice the problem with the chairs. They look as if they are on top of the round table. And they all face the same direction. Let's fix that:

- To make the chairs look like they are under the table, select the chairs ①. Press **Ctrl+B** ②. That shortcut keystroke moves the select object "behind" (or to the background of) other objects in the drawing. By the way, **Ctrl+F** moves selected objects to the foreground (in front of other objects). If you are used to pressing Ctrl+B to make text bold, you need to use Ctrl+Shift+B in Visio instead.

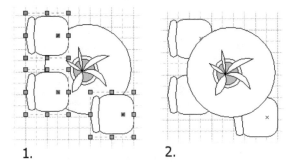

1.   2.

- Rotate the chairs into position. Select a chair. Notice it has a green handle in the center of the seat, called "Rotate Chair" ①. Drag the handle; notice that the chair rotates ②.

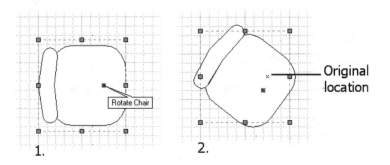

Rotate Chair

Original location

1.   2.

Your floor plan should now look like the following illustration.

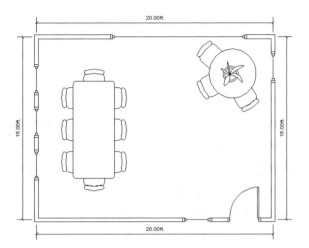

Step 12. The floor plan is mostly complete. You can add finishing touches, such as:

- Center the floor plan on the page with the Tools | Center Drawing command.
- Include a border and title block with the File | Stencil | Visio Extras | Borders & Titles command.
- Add more dimensions by dragging the Dimension Line master from the Office Layout Shapes stencil onto the page, then positioning the dimension.
- Include inventory data by selecting each piece of furniture and using the Shape | Custom Properties command.
- Label the room with the Text tool.

Save your floor plan. A copy of this drawing can be found on the companion CD-ROM under the name Ch 9 - Floorplan diagram tutorial.vsd.

Useful Techniques

The Opening Drawer

Some of the shapes in the Office Layout Shapes stencil contain hidden features. Take, for example, the File shape. When you drag it onto the page, notice that it has an extra handle. ① Dragging the handle pulls the drawer out! ② Other shapes also have hidden features:

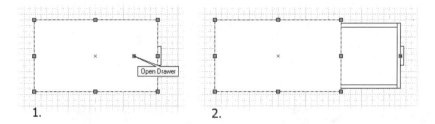

1. 2.

- **Chair** and **Desk Chair:** Rotate the chair.
- **Corner Surface 1** and **3:** Adjust the shape and depth.
- **Corner Surface 2:** Adjust the corner radius.
- **Curved Panel:** Change the radius of the curve.
- **Door** and **Window:** Change the width.
- **File** and **Lateral File:** Open the drawer.
- **Sofa:** Adjust the width of the back and arms.

Advanced: Making a Web Page

In this advanced tutorial, you export the floor plan as a Web page, then view it in a Web browser. Ensure that Visio is still open from the basic tutorial.

Step 1. We'll first add some Web site addresses as hyperlinks:

- Select the conference table, and press **Ctrl+K**. Notice the Hyperlinks dialog box.
- Enter a Web address, such as http://www.steelcase.com shown in the illustration. Click **OK**.

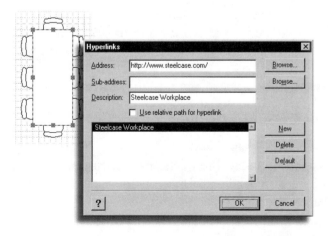

■ Repeat for the chairs. Hold down the **Ctrl** key and select all three chairs. Press **Ctrl+K** and use http://www.hermanmiller.com as the address.

Step 2. Export the drawing as a Web page, as follows:

■ From the menu, select **File | Save As**. Notice the Save As dialog box.

■ In the Save as type list, select "HTML Files (*.htm, *.html)."

■ Click **Save**. Notice the Save As HTML dialog box. The many options available in this dialog box can be imposing to the neophyte. Fortunately, all the default values are exactly what we need.

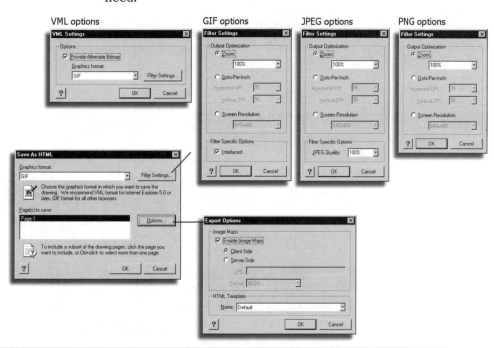

TIP: File formats for the Web   Visio diagrams are not displayed on the Internet. Instead, the diagram is converted to another format, which Web browsers are able to display. Visio's Save As HTML option converts the diagram to one of four image formats, as summarized in the following chart, and surrounds the image with HTML and JavaScript code.

Abbreviation	Meaning	Comments	
GIF	Graphics Interchange Format	Invented by:	CompuServe http://documents.cfar.umd.edu/imageproc/gif89a.doc
		Type:	Lossless raster
		Pros:	Most commonly used format for the Internet. Does not lose any detail when compressed.
		Con:	Use may require a $5,000 license fee from Unisys.
JPEG	Joint Photographic Experts Group	Invented by:	JPEG Committee http://www.jpeg.org/public/jpeghomepage.htm
		Type:	Lossy raster
		Pros:	Creates the smallest raster images. Second most popular format for the Internet.
		Con:	Loses details due to compression method.
PNG	Portable Network Graphics	Invented by:	An informal Internet working group led by Thomas Boutell http://www.libpng.org/pub/png/
		Type:	Lossless raster
		Pros:	Does not lose any detail when compressed. May replace GIF in popularity in coming years.
		Con:	Not (yet) commonly used on the Internet.
VML	Vector Markup Language	Invented by:	Autodesk, HP, MacroMedia, Visio, and Microsoft http://www.w3.org/TR/NOTE-VML
		Type:	Vector
		Pros:	Allows you to zoom and pan the image. Does not lose resolution as image is enlarged. More compact than raster formats.
		Con:	Not displayable by most Web browsers, other than Internet Explorer v5.x

■ Wait a minute or so as Visio generates the image files, along with HTML and JavaScript code. Notice that Visio asks, "Would you like to see the generated pages?" Click **Yes**. Visio launches your computer's default Web browser, and displays the diagram.

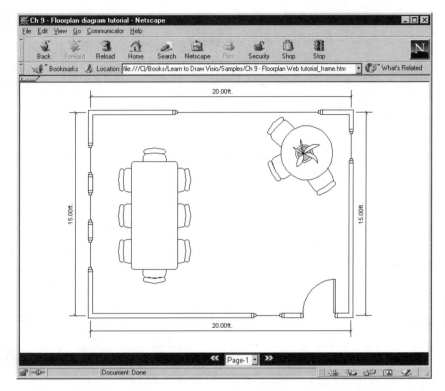

Step 3. Move the cursor over the conference table and the three chairs. Notice that the cursor reports the presence of the links to Steelcase and Herman Miller. If your computer has a connection to the Internet, you can click the furniture and go to those Web sites.

You can find the Web version of the floor plan on the companion CD-ROM under Ch 9 - Floorplan Web tutorial.htm.

TIP: Additional Web features When your Visio diagram contains multiple pages, Visio will optionally export all the pages you specify in the Save As HTML dialog box. In that case, you can view the pages in the Web browser by selecting the page name at the bottom of the screen.

If you have Internet Explorer v5.x, you can save the Visio diagram in VML format. The advantage is that you can pan (using scroll bars) and zoom the image as close as 1200%. The illustration on the following page shows the floor plan zoomed to 400%. The floor plan drawing is available in VML format on the companion CD-ROM under Ch 9 - Floorplan Web VML.htm.

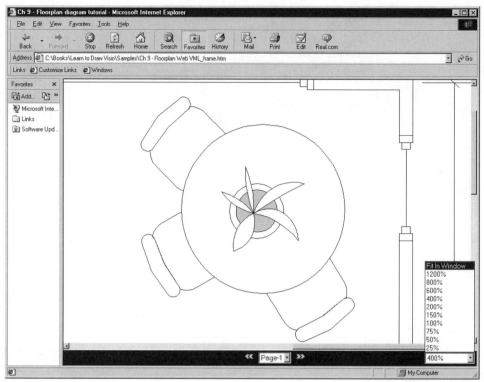

Visio Resources

Visio 2000 provides the following resources for creating floor plans. The templates and stencils are found in the \Visio 2000\Solutions\Office Layout folder.

Related Templates

Office Layout.Vst

Related Stencils

Office Layout Shapes.Vss

Related Commands

Tools | Export Office Inventory

Creates a report of all office equipment in three formats: plain ASCII, Excel spreadsheet, and Access database.

Related Toolbars and Menus

The Snap & Glue toolbar allows you to snap to geometric points, such as the midpoint of a line and the center of an ellipse.

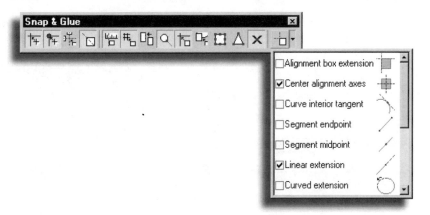

The Architecture menu item provides options for specifying the properties of walls, doors, windows, and spaces, and converting shapes to walls.

Additional Resources

The Standard, Professional, and Enterprise editions of Visio 2000 provide rudimentary support for diagramming floor plans. If you work a lot with floor plans, consider Visio 2000 Technical Edition. Additional functions include:

■ **Space Planning:** Useful for planning; space plans show the rough areas of rooms, halls, plumbing, and other spaces.

■ **Additional Templates:** Electrical, telecommunications, landscaping, furniture, and reflected ceiling plans.

■ **Facilities Management:** Helps you track and manage facilities data. Links to SQL databases.

■ **HVAC:** Allows you to create diagrams of heating, ventilating, and air conditioning systems. Ductwork shapes rotate, align, and snap automatically to each other.

- **CAD Export:** Exports the Visio drawing in a variety of CAD formats, including DWG (AutoCAD and IntelliCAD), DXF (many other desktop CAD systems), DGN (MicroStation), and IGES (many industrial CAD systems).

For more information, see http://www.visio.com/visio2000/technical/.

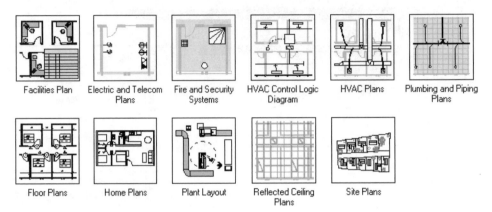

| Facilities Plan | Electric and Telecom Plans | Fire and Security Systems | HVAC Control Logic Diagram | HVAC Plans | Plumbing and Piping Plans |

| Floor Plans | Home Plans | Plant Layout | Reflected Ceiling Plans | Site Plans |

Summary

In this chapter, you learned how to create a floor plan, then export it as a Web page.

Quiz

1. The purpose of scale in a drawing is to:
   a. Measure the size of the page.
   b. Make the drawing fit the page.
   c. Measure the file size of the diagram.
   d. Make the Visio file fit the hard disk.

2. How many inches are there in a foot?
   a. 12"
   b. 10"
   c. 25.4"
   d. 3.038"

3. How wide is the typical margin (the area where printers cannot print)?
   a. 11"
   b. ½"
   c. ¼"
   d. 0"

4. Spaces can be converted to walls and back again.
   True / False

5. A dimension indicates:
   a. Distances.
   b. Lengths and angles.
   c. All of the above.
   d. None of the above.

6. Match the shortcut keystroke with its meaning:
   a. Ctrl+B   i.   Insert hyperlink.
   b. Ctrl+F   ii.   Make text bold.
   c. Ctrl+Shift+B   iii. Move object to the background.
   d. Ctrl+K   iv.   Move object to the foreground.

7. At a scale of ¼" = 1', a line 2" long on the page represents a line in the real world of length:
   a. 2"
   b. 12"
   c. 48"
   d. 96"

8. The zero point of Visio's two rulers cannot be repositioned.
   True / False

9. The problem of using JPEG images to represent a Visio drawing is:
   a. All colors are converted to gray.
   b. Details can be lost.
   c. They are not displayed by most Web browsers.
   d. They may require payment of a royalty fee.

10. One advantage of using VML to represent a Visio drawing on the Web is:

    a.   The ability to zoom and pan the image without loss of resolution.

    b.   It is the most popular format on the Internet.

    c.   It can be displayed by Netscape Navigator and Opera Web browsers.

    d.   It is a raster format.

Exercises

1. How large a building can be diagrammed on a 17" x 11" sheet of paper at a scale of ½"=1'? Allow a quarter-inch margin along all edges of the paper. Express your answer in feet.

2. Open the Ch 9 - Floorplan diagram tutorial.vsd file found on the companion CD-ROM. Add a second room and furniture. If necessary, use the Page Setup command to enlarge the drawing area.

3. Continuing the floor plan created in exercise #2, add dimensions to the room. Change the wall thickness to 6".

4. Create a floor plan of your bedroom, to scale. If you are feeling adventurous, diagram your entire home.

5. Using the floor plan created in exercise #4, export the diagram as an HTML document using GIF for the image type.

Isometric and CAD Drawings

What are Isometric and CAD Drawings?

When you create a Visio diagram, it is flat (two-dimensional, or "2-D" for short). Indeed, most drawings created by any graphics package are 2-D, whether diagrammed in Visio, drawn by a paint program, or drafted with CAD software. Two-dimensional drawings, however, can be hard to read; for most laypeople, a 3-D drawing is easier to view.

Over the centuries, drafters have developed methods to simulate 3-D views. You are probably most familiar with perspective drawings, which simulate depth of field with a vanishing viewpoint. The problem with perspective drawings is that they cannot be dimensioned.

Visio provides a solution for creating perspective diagrams: see the Blocks with Perspective stencil in the \Visio 2000\Solutions\Block Diagram folder. (The diagrams are not, however, truly perspective; it would be more accurate to call them *orthographic* diagrams.)

In this chapter, you learn about:

- Displaying a CAD drawing in a Visio diagram
- Converting a CAD drawing into shapes
- Creating an isometric grid
- Drawing isometric cubes and circles

187

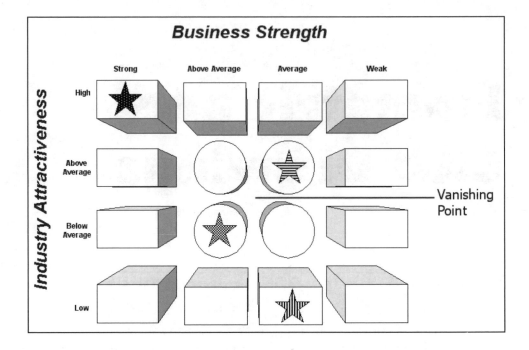

Another form of 3-D simulation is called the *isometric drawing*. In this form of drawing, you see the left and right sides and top of objects, each slanted at a 60-degree angle. You probably recognize the word from isometric triangle, which is a triangle with equal sides, and three 60-degree corners. "Isometric" is based on the Latin word *iso*, which means "same." Visio does not provide any solutions for creating isometric drawings, although an isometric P&ID (piping and instrumentation drawing) solution is available from third-party developers.

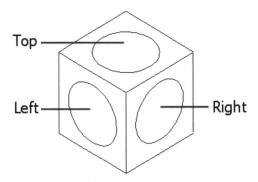

CAD Drawings

The most accurate drawings are created by CAD software. *CAD* is short for "computer-aided design." CAD drawings are the basis for constructing every-thing from buildings, airports, and automobiles to toasters. The most popular

CAD packages are AutoCAD and MicroStation. Visio used to sell its own CAD package, called IntelliCAD 98. Just before Visio was purchased by Microsoft, Visio handed the IntelliCAD 2000 source code over to the IntelliCAD Technical Consortium. All editions of Visio 2000 are able to read drawings created by the following CAD programs:

File Format	Meaning
DWG	Short for DraWinG.
	Native file format of AutoCAD (and derivative products, such as AutoCAD LT), IntelliCAD, and Vdraft.
	This binary-format file is not documented by Autodesk; much of the format has been documented by the OpenDWG Alliance.
DGN	Short for DesiGN.
	Native file format of MicroStation, based on the IGDS format created by Intergraph (Interactive Graphics Design System).
	This ASCII-format file has only the original IGDS portions documented.
DXF	Short for drawing interchange format.
	This ASCII-format file is the plain-text version of DWG developed by Autodesk for third-party developers to extract data from DWG files.
	Largely documented by Autodesk, although some parts are encrypted, such as ACIS data.
IGES	Short for Initial Graphics Exchange Specification.
	This ASCII-format file was designed by a committee for exchanging drawings between different CAD packages; superceded by the all-encompassing PDES/STEP.
	Fully documented by the National Institute of Standards and Technology (www.nist.gov).

Only Visio 2000 Technical Edition is able to convert a Visio diagram into those four file formats. A bug in the Save As dialog box makes it appear that other editions of Visio can convert to CAD formats, but this is not the case. For more information on CAD products and file formats, visit these Web sites:

Product	Source	Web Site
CAD Products		
AutoCAD	Autodesk	www.autodesk.com
MicroStation	Bentley Systems	www.bentley.com
IntelliCAD	IntelliCAD Technical Consortium	www.intellicad.org

Lesson 10

Product	Source	Web Site
Vdraft	SoftSource	www.vdraft.com
File Formats		
DWG File Format	OpenDWG Alliance	www.opendwg.org/downloads/guest.html#dwgspec
DXF File Format	Autodesk	www3.autodesk.com/adsk/support/item/0,,140239—125452,00.html
IGES File Format	National Institute of Standards and Technology	www.nist.gov/iges/
IGDS File Format	Intergraph	www.intergraph.com

Tutorials

In the following tutorials, you learn how to display a CAD drawing, and how to create isometric drawings.

Basic: Displaying a CAD Drawing

In this basic tutorial, you learn how to open a drawing created by a CAD package, such as AutoCAD, IntelliCAD, or MicroStation.

Step 1. Start Visio. When the Welcome to Visio 2000 dialog box appears, double-click the **Choose drawing type** option.

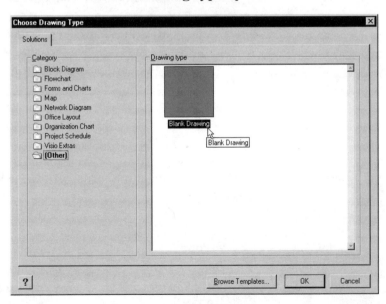

Step 2. In the Category section of the Choose Drawing Type dialog box, click **(Other)**, and then double-click the **Blank Drawing** option. Notice that Visio opens a new blank drawing.

Step 3. From the menu bar, select **Insert | CAD Drawing**. Notice the Insert CAD Drawing dialog box.

Step 4. Select the **Ch10 - DWG Drawing.dwg** file found on the companion CD-ROM. Click **Open**. Notice the CAD Drawing Properties dialog box.

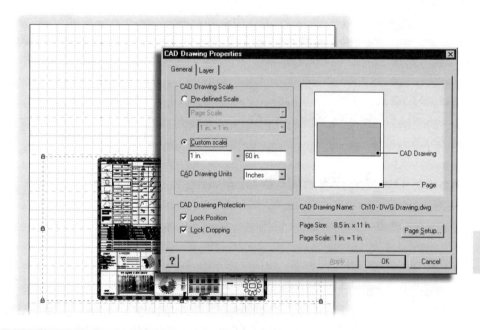

TIP: Displaying CAD images   When you drag the CAD Drawing Properties dialog box out of the way, you will see that Visio has already displayed an image of the CAD drawing on the page.

Step 5. You have two choices here: (1) You can accept all the defaults, and click **OK**; or (2) you can fiddle with the settings, some of which can be quite difficult to comprehend. In my experience, the Visio user usually does not know how the CAD drawing was constructed, and hence doesn't know which options to select. In the following description of the dialog box options, the ◈ symbol indicates which choice to make when you don't know anything about the incoming CAD drawing.

Lesson 10

General Tab

CAD Drawing Scale Area

Pre-defined Scale: Specifies preset drawing scales based on industry standards, including Architectural, Civil Engineering, Metric, and Mechanical Engineering. Select the scale factor from the second list, such as 1/8"=1' or 1"=10'0". Notice that Visio previews the size of the scaled drawing in the dialog box.

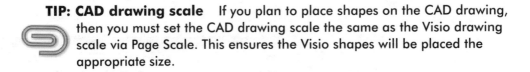

TIP: CAD drawing scale   If you plan to place shapes on the CAD drawing, then you must set the CAD drawing scale the same as the Visio drawing scale via Page Scale. This ensures the Visio shapes will be placed the appropriate size.

Custom scale: Allows you to enter any scale factor. The dialog box initially sets this option, because Visio automatically scales the CAD drawing to fit the page. ◈ Select Custom scale if you are not sure about the scale.

CAD Drawing Units: Specifies how to interpret CAD drawing units. CAD drawings are always drawn full-size (never to scale) in either inches or meters, in most cases. This list box lets you select the units in which the CAD drawing was created, including miles and millimeters. ◈ If you are not sure, select Inches.

CAD Drawing Protection Area

Lock Position: When on, prevents you from moving the CAD drawing on the page. When off, you can relocate the drawing with the Pointer tool. ◈ Turn off this option.

Lock Cropping: When on, prevents you from cropping or panning a cropped CAD drawing. When off, you can crop and pan the drawing with the Crop tool. ◈ Turn off this option.

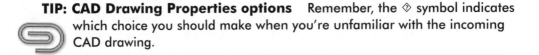

TIP: CAD Drawing Properties options   Remember, the ◈ symbol indicates which choice you should make when you're unfamiliar with the incoming CAD drawing.

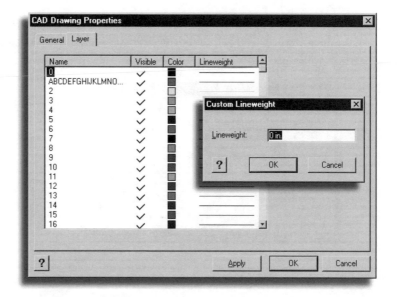

Layer Tab

Name: Lists the names of layers found in the CAD drawing. All objects in a CAD drawing are assigned to one layer. This is different from Visio, where shapes can be assigned to no layer, or to more than one layer. Some CAD packages display numbers for their layer names. MicroStation drawings, in particular, are limited to 63 layers numbered from 1 to 63. You cannot edit the name of the layer in Visio.

Visible: When on, a check mark shows. When visible, the objects on the CAD layer are displayed by Visio. When off, the objects are not displayed. ◇ Leave all layers visible.

Color: Specifies the color assigned to the layer by the CAD software. You can click the color to display the Windows standard Color dialog box, and choose another color. In some cases, however, this does not change the color displayed by the objects. The reason is that the CAD drafter may have overridden the layer color by assigning a color to the objects themselves. ◇ Do not change colors.

TIP: Layer colors   Technically, a CAD program does not assign a color to layers and objects. Instead, it assigns a number, which, in turn, refers to a color. In AutoCAD, for example, color #1 is red. In MicroStation, however, color #1 is blue. If Visio appears to display the wrong colors, it is because the color matching is incorrect.

Lineweight: Specifies the lineweight (thickness) assigned to the layer by the CAD software. You can click the line to display the Custom Lineweight dialog box, and enter another width. ◈ Do not change lineweights.

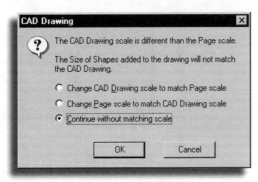

Step 6.   Click **OK**. When you select a custom scale, Visio may display the CAD Drawing dialog box, which complains about the scale. The dialog box gives you three options:

- **Change CAD Drawing scale to match Page scale**. This makes the CAD drawing small enough to fit the page.

- **Change Page scale to match CAD Drawing scale**. This makes the page large enough to encompass the entire CAD drawing.

- **Continue without matching scale**. This makes no change to either the CAD drawing or the page. ◈ Don't match scale, unless you have a need to do so.

Click **OK**. Notice the CAD drawing. This is a special drawing because it displays every object found in an AutoCAD Release 14 drawing. You can use this to check the accuracy of drawing translations; compare the drawing as displayed by AutoCAD with the drawing displayed by Visio.

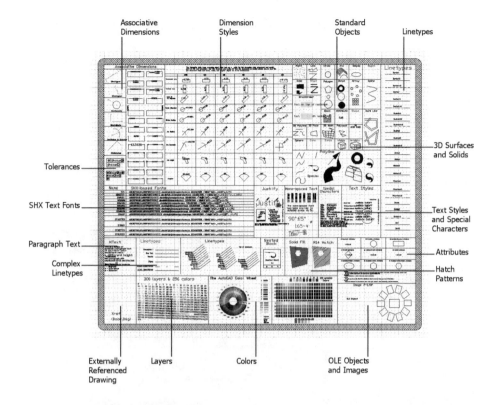

Step 7.   To make changes to the drawing, right-click the drawing and select **CAD Drawing | Properties**. Notice that the CAD Drawing Properties dialog box is identical to the one you saw upon first inserting the drawing. Make changes, and click **OK**.

Step 8.   To convert the CAD drawing to Visio shapes, right-click the drawing and select **CAD Drawing | Convert**. Notice the Convert Wizard, which guides you through three steps of selecting options.

WARNING: It can take an hour to convert a moderate-size CAD drawing to Visio shapes. In addition, the conversion is not 100% accurate. Objects may appear different or they may be missing altogether.

- **Select the layers to convert.** You can have Visio convert the objects found on specific layers or on all layers (the default). To select one layer, click its name. To select more than one layer, hold down the Ctrl key as you click layer names. To select a range of layers, hold down the Shift key as you click the first and last layer name in the range. ◈ Convert all layers.

Lesson 10

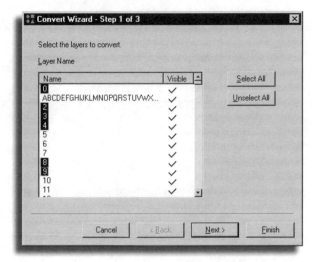

- **Delete converted layers.** You have the option of deleting unneeded layers. ◇ Delete selected DWG layers.

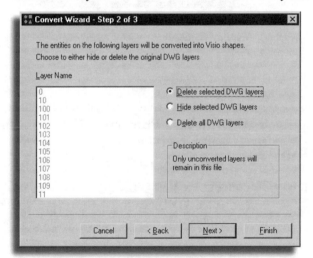

- **Convert dimensions.** The dimensions found in the CAD drawing can be converted to dimension shapes or into lines and text. ◇ Convert to Visio dimension shapes.

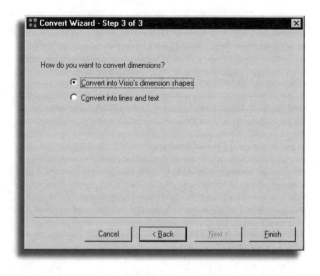

Click **Finish.** Notice that Visio spends a lot of time converting the drawing.

TIP: Conversion alternative An alternative to the Convert command is to use the Ungroup command. I find this is more efficient for small drawings. Select the drawing, then press Ctrl+U. This converts the CAD objects into Visio shapes. After conversion, I find it useful to collect the shapes into a group with Ctrl+G.

Useful Techniques

Displaying DWG in Visio

All editions of Visio 2000 can read DWG and DXF files to display drawings created by AutoCAD and compatible CAD packages. Visio 2000 uses the IntelliCAD DWG engine to perform the display. Visio 2000 does not, however, display the following objects:

- 2-D and 3-D objects created with ACIS. This includes 2-D regions and 3-D solids.
- Proxy objects (a.k.a. zombie objects)
- OLE objects
- Image (raster) objects
- Some text is not justified correctly, such as Aligned and Fit modes.
- The shapes are missing from complex linetypes.

- TrueType fonts are displayed as SHX vector fonts.
- Rays and xlines are cut off at the drawing extents.

Converting DWG to Visio

When converting the AutoCAD drawing to Visio format (via the CAD Drawing | Convert command), Visio 2000 makes the following errors:

- Splines are not 100% identical.
- R12-style non-associative dimensions are wrong scale.
- SHX fonts are changed to Arial TrueType font, with the exception of RomanD and RomanC SHX fonts, which are converted to Times New Roman TrueType font.
- Complex linetypes are changed into continuous lines.
- Text styles (vertical, oblique, backwards, width factor) are lost.
- The text overline and underline are not displayed; other special characters are handled correctly, although the %%%% code is interpreted incorrectly.
- Some text has massive spacing between characters, stretching a single word across the entire page.
- Attributes are not displayed.
- R12-style non-associative hatch patterns are broken into individual line segments.
- Associative hatch patterns are not displayed.

The following objects are not displayed after conversion:

- 2-D and 3-D objects created with ACIS. This includes 2-D regions and 3-D solids.
- Proxy objects (a.k.a. zombie objects)
- OLE objects
- Image (raster) objects
- Rays and xlines are cut off at the drawing extents.

Converting Visio to DWG

Only Visio Technical can convert Visio drawings into CAD format. Here are some issues to be aware of:

DWG or DXF. There is no difference between conversion to DWG or DXF format. DWG is read by AutoCAD, IntelliCAD, Vdraft, MicroStation, and several other CAD packages; DXF is read by a broader range of non-CAD software. Both formats will create the same list of inaccuracies.

Visio v5.x's drawing converter allowed some mapping. This has been removed from Visio 2000 to make things "simpler." I think the philosophy behind Visio 2000's support for DWG was that it primarily be for background images rather than actual conversion.

Shapes That Don't Convert. If a shape will not convert properly to AutoCAD, the problem may lie in it being a group. The shapes included with Visio Network Equipment, for example, often do not convert to DWG. The solution is to ungroup the shape, as follows:

Step 1. Select all objects with **Ctrl+A**.

Step 2. Ungroup with **Ctrl+U**.

Step 3. Repeat 1 and 2 until no groups exist.

Step 4. Save as DWG or DXF.

Step 5. Exit Visio—DON'T save the Visio drawing!

Linetypes. Many of Visio's complex or custom linetypes translate a single, continuous line in AutoCAD. Sometimes, the linetype pattern is translated incompletely.

Text. If the text is "too long," it can be fixed in AutoCAD by re-specifying the style (via AutoCAD's Style command) with a narrower font or a narrower width factor, such as 0.85. By default, Visio text is translated to AutoCAD's TXT font.

Sometimes Visio text blocks appear rotated by 180 degrees in AutoCAD. Use AutoCAD's Rotate command to turn around the text.

You might find that a Visio character cannot be matched in the AutoCAD font. AutoCAD then displays the character with a question mark (?). A common example is the Visio tab character, which is not supported by AutoCAD.

Visio fails to underline and overline text when importing from DWG. The same problem occurs on the way back to AutoCAD: text underlined in Visio is not underlined in AutoCAD, even though AutoCAD supports underlining.

Other Issues. Visio converts all arrowheads to an AutoCAD 2-D solid object, which means that arrowheads are filled in, whether or not they were filled in Visio.

Images (bitmaps) are not converted, even though AutoCAD can display them.

Lineweights are not correctly displayed, even though AutoCAD 2000 can display them.

If a solid fill is missing, AutoCAD 2000 can be used to fill an area with a white color using the BHatch command.

Visio Support of CAD Drawings

The #1 problem I get asked about is translation of drawing files between AutoCAD (and perhaps IntelliCAD) and Visio. While users find that Visio 2000 is faster, they are disappointed that it provides less control over the translation than did Visio v5.x. What are needed, of course, are improvements to the DWG/DXF translator from Microsoft. These changes are, however, unlikely to occur.

The word is that Microsoft doesn't care to cross swords with Autodesk, and has begun to de-emphasize DWG translation in Visio. As this book was being written, I received news that the recent move by Microsoft was to pull all (but five) SHX fonts. One reason for the de-emphasis may be financial: according to the most recent figures I have, Visio Technical made up just 15% of total Visio sales. IntelliCAD 98 cost Visio US$25 million, but sold just 25,000 copies; the company ended up giving away IntelliCAD. These are the sort of numbers that would make upper management consider pulling out of a market segment, especially a segment as tough to break into as CAD.

Microsoft, the new owner of Visio, is hot on XML (short for eXtended Markup Language, an extension to HTML). Microsoft plans to move the next major release of Visio to XML. The master plan for Visio is to emphasize IT (information technology) and de-emphasize technical drawing. On the one hand, XML seems like a natural extension considering that Visio Professional, Visio Enterprise, and VNE (Visio Network Equipment) are all IT oriented. On the other hand, this is a far cry from the "Master Plan" that Visio outlined several years ago:

- Visio Technical was to be marketed for technical drawing, and Phoenix (as IntelliCAD was known back then) for 2-D/3-D drafting. This happened until the 2000 series was released.

- Visio would borrow from Phoenix for better AutoCAD compatibility. This has happened in Visio 2000.

- Solids modeling, which was thought to represent 10% of the market, would be left to a high-end partner, such as SolidWorks. Visio planned to include hooks to display 3-D solids in Phoenix. This never happened, and there are no plans to ever display 3-D solids in Visio.

- Visio wanted to become the single standard for creating, storing, and exchanging technical drawings. It would now appear that this goal is being abandoned.

At the 1998 Visio Solutions Conference, Visio moved the goalposts, declaring that it wanted to become "the single worldwide standard for business drawing." Note the change in adjective, from "technical" to "business." Nevertheless, Visio added powerful tools for P&ID (piping and instrumentation diagramming), for which Visio is a superior product to AutoCAD. They also added support for MicroStation DGN files. Visio 2000 also allows all editions to read CAD format files.

The 1999 Visio Solutions Conference gave the first indication that CAD was in trouble at Visio: there were no sessions for IntelliCAD. Visio's excuse was that the conference focus was on VBA (the Visual Basic for Applications macro language), a weak excuse since IntelliCAD included VBA. Perhaps by then Visio had already decided to unload IntelliCAD, which was announced later in 1999 and within weeks of Visio announcing it would sell itself to Microsoft. Coincidence? Visio insists it was, but I remain unconvinced.

So we now have the situation of firms buying into Visio, finding it works well for highly structured technical diagrams, but are not happy with its DWG compatibility. The move by Microsoft to pull most AutoCAD-compatible SHX fonts will only worsen the situation. This means that drawing translation will be less accurate than ever before. While SHX fonts may be a minor issue to the millions of Visio users, the accurate display of text is crucial in a CAD drawing, especially when the drawing is a legal document, more so than in a typical word processing document.

Advanced: Making an Isometric Drawing

In this advanced tutorial, you create an isometric grid of guidelines, then draw an isometric cube with isometric circles. Visio does not include an isometric grid (as do CAD programs), so you need to create it, as follows:

Step 1.   Start a new Visio drawing.

Step 2.   You'll find it easier if the grid lies on its own layer. From the menu bar, select **View | Layer Properties**. In the dialog box, create the following settings:

- Name   **Isogrid**
- Visible   ✓
- Print   (Isometric gridlines will not be printed.)
- Active   ✓ (Guidelines will be placed on this layer.)
- Lock
- Snap   ✓

- Glue   ✓
- Color   ✓
- Layer Color   **15** (Light gray color is faintly visible.)

Click **OK**.

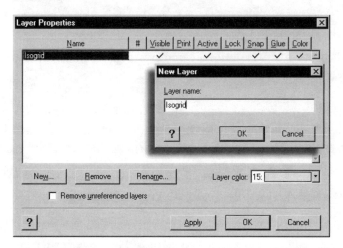

Step 3. We won't need the regular grid, because we are creating the new isometric grid. From the menu bar, select **View | Grid** to turn off the display of the rectangular grid.

Step 4. To start creating the isometric grid, we need to rotate the page by 60 degrees. Select the **Rotation** tool.

Step 5. Grab the corner of the page, and rotate the page counterclockwise. Keep an eye on the status line; stop rotating when you see Angle = 60 degrees.

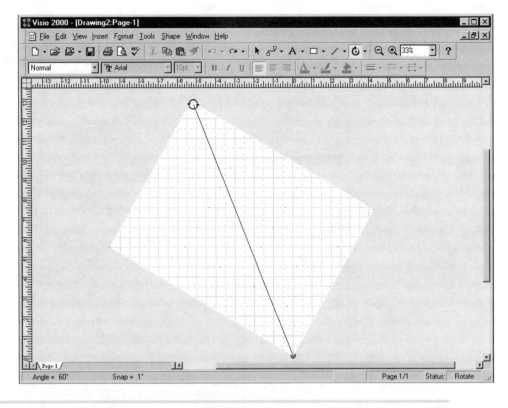

TIP: Enabling rotation   If the page does not rotate, the option is turned off. To turn on the option, select **Tools | Options**. Select the **Drawing tab**, and click **Enable page rotation**. Click **OK**.

Step 6. Select the **Pointer** tool.

Step 7. Drag a guideline from the vertical ruler to the closest corner of the page. (If the ruler is not visible, select **View | Rulers**.)

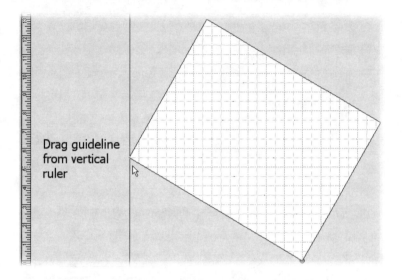

Step 8. Hold down the **Ctrl** key, and make a copy of the guideline. Drag the guideline 0.5 inches to the left. Keep an eye on the status line or ruler.

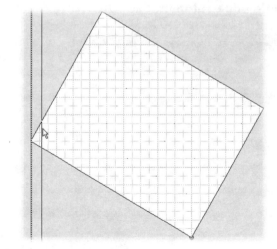

Step 9. Press function key **F4.** Notice that Visio makes a copy of the guideline 0.5 inches to the left. Keep pressing F4 until the entire page is covered with vertical guidelines spaced 0.5 inches apart.

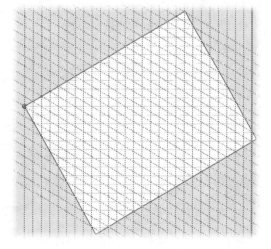

Step 10. You have now created one set of guidelines. You create two more sets, each at 60 degrees to one another. Repeat the previous steps:

- Select the **Rotation** tool.
- Drag the page clockwise until the status line reads –60 degrees.
- Select the **Pointer** tool.
- Drag a guideline from the vertical ruler to the corner of the page.
- Hold down the **Ctrl** key and make a copy of the guideline, 0.5 inches to the left.
- Press the **F4** key to add the remaining guidelines.

- Select the **Rotation** tool, and drag the page counterclockwise until the status line reads 0 degrees.

- Zoom into the page with **Ctrl+Shift** to get a close-up view of the diamond-like pattern.

- Select the **Pointer** tool, and drag a guideline from the vertical ruler. Ensure that the new guideline matches the top and bottom of the "diamonds."

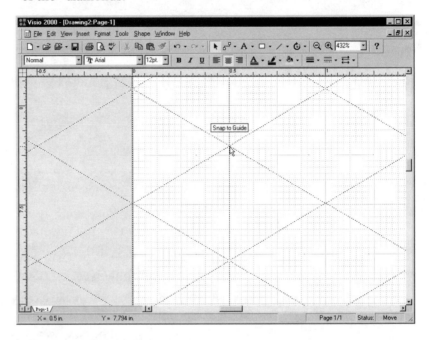

- Hold down the **Ctrl** and make a copy of the guideline, 0.5 inches to the left. Press the **F4** key to add the remaining guidelines.

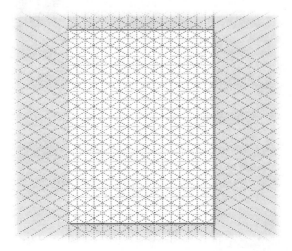

Step 11. Save your valuable work with **Ctrl+S**. You can find this drawing on the companion CD-ROM under the name Ch10 - Isometric grid.vsd.

Step 12. With the isometric grid set up, we need to change layers. From the menu bar, select **View | Layer Properties**. In the dialog box:

- For layer Isogrid, click **Active** to turn it off.
- Create a new layer named **0** (zero).
- For layer 0, click **Active** to turn it on.

Click **OK** to dismiss the dialog box.

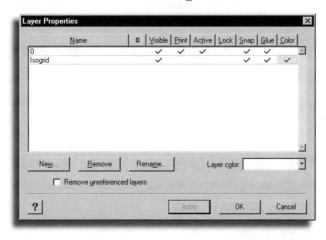

Step 13. Let's try drawing some isometric shapes. First, a cube:

- Select the **Line** tool.
- Start drawing a line from the intersection of three guidelines.
- Draw three lines from 1 to 2, 2 to 3, and 3 to 4, as shown below.

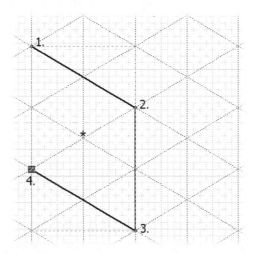

■ Draw a fourth line from 4 to 1. Notice that Visio creates a solid parallelogram. This is the left side of the isometric cube.

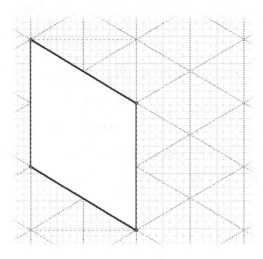

■ Repeat to draw the right side of the cube. Notice that you need to draw all four lines: from 1 to 2, 2 to 3, 3 to 4, and back to 1 again.

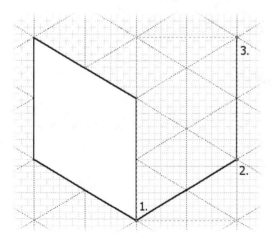
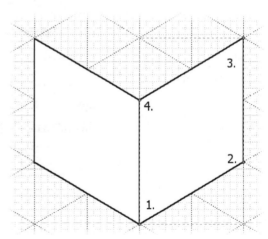

■ Finally, draw the top of the cube.

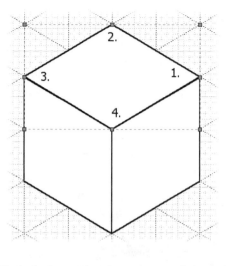

- To help keep the three parts of the cube together, convert the three parallelograms into a group. Hold down the **Ctrl** key and select each shape. Press **Ctrl+G**, and Visio makes the group.

Step 14. To draw a circle in an isometric drawing, you need to draw an ellipse, which is a flattened circle. Visio doesn't provide any tools to create isometric circles (called "isocircle" for short), so follow these steps carefully to draw an isocircle on the top plane:

- Select the **Ellipse** tool.

- To draw an isocircle on the top of the cube, start at the center of the edge shown in the illustration ①.

- Drag the ellipse to the opposite side ②.

- If necessary, adjust the size of the isocircle.

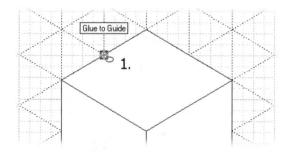
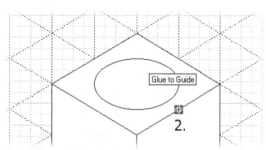

Step 15. Drawing isocircles on the left and right planes requires an extra step. The isocircle needs to be rotated, as follows:

- To help with the rotation, open the Size & Position window. From the menu bar, select **View | Windows | Size & Position**.

■ Make a copy of the isocircle: hold down the **Ctrl** key, and drag the isocircle to the left plane ①. Notice that the isocircle looks "wrong."

■ Rotate the isocircle: in the Size & Position window's Angle field, enter **–60** and press **Enter** ②. Notice that the isocircle now looks correct.

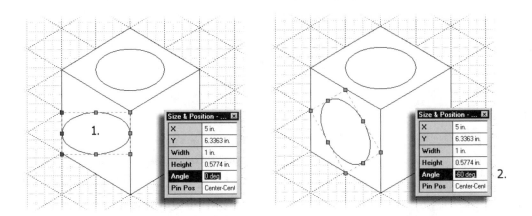

■ Repeat for the isocircle on the right side face of the cube. This time, however, enter **60** for the angle.

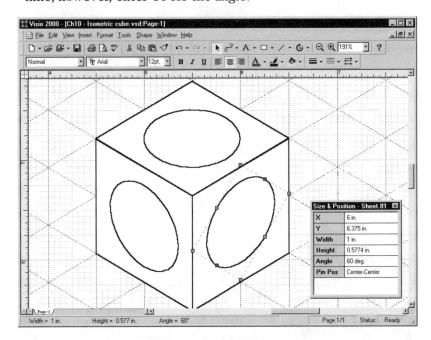

Placing isometric text is harder, since the font needs to be created first. Visio, on its own, is unable to create the font style required for isometric text. That's because the text needs to have an obliquing (sloping characters) angle of 30 degrees.

Save your work. This diagram can be found on the companion CD-ROM under the name Ch10 - Isometric cube.vsd.

TIP: Making isometric stencils   Since isometric shapes can be difficult to draw, make use of Visio's stencils. After you draw an isometric shape that you might reuse, drag it onto a new stencil.

Visio Resources

Visio 2000 provides some resources for working with CAD drawings and creating isometric diagrams. The following files are found in the Visio Extras folder.

Related Templates

In the \Visio 2000\Solutions\Visio Extras Folder

_dwgcnvt.vst—Template for converting AutoCAD DWG and DXF files.
_dgncnvt.vst—Template for converting MicroStation DGN files.

Related Menus

The File and Insert items on the menu bar contain commands for accessing CAD drawings:

- **File | Open** opens a new Visio diagram with the CAD drawing.
- **Insert | CAD Drawing** adds a CAD drawing to an existing diagram.

Lesson 10

The right-click menu contains two commands for modifying CAD drawings:

■ **CAD Drawing | Convert** converts all or part of the CAD drawing to Visio shapes.

■ **CAD Drawing | Properties** changes the properties of the CAD drawing, such as its scale, layer colors, and display of layers.

Related Files

In the \Visio 2000\Samples\Visio Extras Folder

The following sample files are available for testing the CAD drawing conversion in Visio:

floorplan.dwg—Sample AutoCAD DWG file.
floorplan.dgn—Sample MicroStation DGN file.

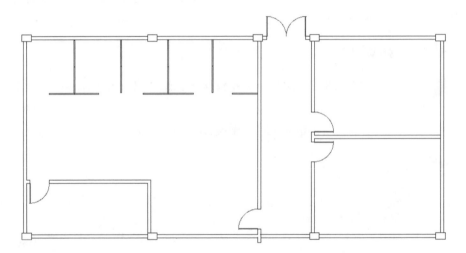

Summary

In this chapter, you learned how to import a CAD drawing into Visio, and how to create an isometric drawing.

Quiz

1. An isometric drawing:
    a.   Contains three pages.
    b.   Contains three views.
    c.   Simulates 3-D in a 2-D environment.
    d.   Consists of triangles.

2. Match the abbreviation with its meaning:

   a. 2-D   i.   Computer-aided design

   b. 3-D   ii.   Two dimensional

   c. DWG   iii. Drawing file

   d. DXF   iv.   Three dimensional

   e. CAD   v.   Drawing interchange file

3. The Custom Scale option of the CAD Drawing Properties dialog box automatically scales the CAD drawing to fit the Visio page.

   True / False

4. The Color option of the CAD Drawing Properties dialog box's Layers tab always changes the color of the selected layer.

   True / False

5. Lineweight specifies:

   a. Width of lines.

   b. Width of boxes.

   c. Size of the drawing.

   d. Width of the drawing.

6. Once the CAD drawing is inserted in the Visio page, it cannot be changed.

   True / False

7. To rotate the page:

   a. Use the Edit | Page command.

   b. Use the Rotation tool.

   c. Use the Page tool.

   d. Use the File | Page Setup command.

8. An isometric circle is drawn as a:

   a. Circle.

   b. Multi-segment polygon.

   c. Ellipse.

   d. Multi-segment polyline.

9. To draw an isocircle on the front face of an isometric drawing:

   a. Draw an ellipse and rotate it to 60 degrees.

   b. Draw an ellipse and rotate it to –60 degrees.

   c. Draw a circle and rotate it to –60 degrees.

   d. Draw a circle and rotate it to 60 degrees.

10. Visio is able to draw isometric text.

    True / False

Exercises

1. Open the Ch10 - Isometric grid.vsd file found on the companion CD-ROM. Draw an isometric rectangle and place an isocircle on each plane. Using the text tool, label the three isometric planes: top, left, and right.

2. Open the Ch10 - Isometric grid.vsd file found on the companion CD-ROM. Re-create the isometric diagram shown in the illustration.

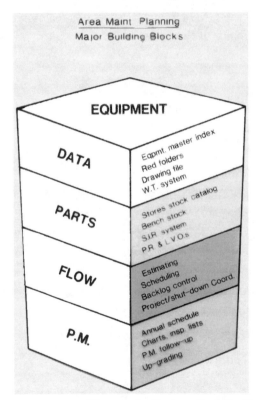

Diagram by Herbert Grabowski

3. Draw the isometric cylinder shown in the illustration.

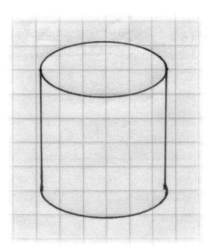

4. Draw the isometric wedge shown in the illustration.

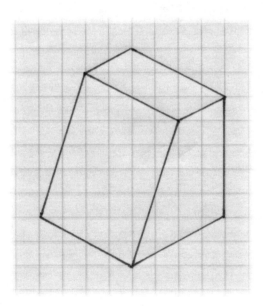

Lesson

5. Draw the isometric bracket shown in the illustration.

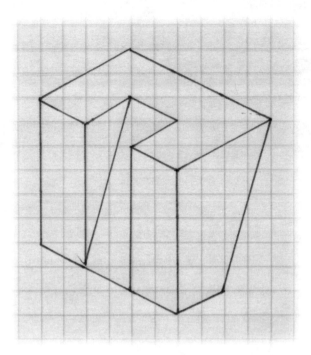

Appendix A

Mouse and Keyboard Shortcuts

You may find that you work more quickly when you use Visio's shortcut keystrokes and mouse button. In this appendix, you find all shortcuts listed two ways: first in alphabetical order by tool name, then in alphabetical order by keystroke. This list is more complete than that provided by Visio 2000's documentation.

Shortcuts by Task

General Tasks

Use the following mouse buttons and keystrokes to perform general tasks:

Select shape	Click
Shortcut menu	Right-click
Customized operation	Double-click
Add to or remove from selection set	Shift + click
Nudge	Select an object, then press cursor keys
Pixel nudge	Select object, Shift, and press cursor keys
Repeat last command	F4
Pointer	Ctrl+1
Exit Visio	Ctrl+Q or Alt+F4

Pan & Zoom

Use the following shortcut keys to quickly zoom and pan your drawing:

Actual Size (100%)	Ctrl+I
Pan	Ctrl+Shift and drag while holding down the right mouse button, or press cursor keys when no objects are selected
Whole Page	Ctrl+W
Open the Zoom dialog box	F6
Zoom in	Ctrl+Shift and click
Zoom out	Shift+F6 or Ctrl+Shift and right-click
Zoom in on an area	Ctrl+Shift and drag a rectangle

Drawing Tools

Use the following shortcut keys to quickly switch between drawing tools:

Arc	Ctrl+7
Connection point	Ctrl+Shift+1
Connector	Ctrl+3
Crop image	Ctrl+Shift+2
Ellipse	Ctrl+9
Freeform	Ctrl+5
Line	Ctrl+6
Pencil	Ctrl+4
Rectangle	Ctrl+8
Rotation	Ctrl+0 (zero)
Stamp	Ctrl+Shift+3
Text	Ctrl+2
Text block	Ctrl+Shift+4
Toggle between text edit and selection mode	Select a shape, then press F2

Menu Commands

For many of these shortcuts, you must select a shape first:

Activate the menu bar	Alt or F10
Align Shapes dialog box	F8
Bring selected shapes to front	Ctrl+F

Cascade windows	Alt+F7
Copy to clipboard	Ctrl+C
Cut to clipboard	Ctrl+X
Duplicate selected shapes	Ctrl+D
Field dialog box	Ctrl+F9
Fill dialog box	F3
Flip horizontal	Ctrl+H
Flip vertical	Ctrl+J
Glue toggle (on or off)	F9
Group selected shapes	Ctrl+G
Help dialog box	F1
Hyperlinks dialog box	Ctrl+K
Line dialog box	Shift+F3
Macros dialog box	Alt+F8
New drawing (based on current drawing)	Ctrl+N
Open dialog box	Ctrl+O
Page dialog box	F5
Paste from clipboard	Ctrl+V
Print dialog box	Ctrl+P
Page Setup dialog box, Print Setup tab	Shift+F5
Redo	Ctrl+Y
Repeat last command	F4
Rotate left	Ctrl+L
Rotate right	Ctrl+R
Save As dialog box	F12
Save drawing	Ctrl+S
Save Workspace dialog box	Alt+F12
Select all	Ctrl+A
Send selected shapes to back	Ctrl+B
Size & Position window	Click the status bar
Snap toggle (on or off)	Shift+F9
Snap & Glue dialog box	Alt+F9
Spelling dialog box	F7

Appendix A

Text dialog box, Font tab	F11
Text dialog box, Paragraph tab	Shift+F11
Text dialog box, Tabs tab	Ctrl+F11
Tile windows horizontally	Shift+F7
Tile windows vertically	Ctrl+Shift+F7
Undo	Ctrl+Z
Ungroup selected groups	Ctrl+U
Visual Basic Editor	Alt+F11

Text Formatting

Use the following key combinations to apply and remove formatting to selected text:

Bold	Ctrl+Shift+B
Italic	Ctrl+Shift+I
Small caps	Ctrl+Shift+Y
Sub$_{script}$	Ctrl+Shift+X
Super^{script}	Ctrl+Shift+Z
Underline	Ctrl+Shift+U

Special Text Characters

Use the following key combinations to add special characters in text:

Beginning single quote '	Ctrl+[
Ending single quote '	Ctrl+]
Beginning double quote "	Ctrl+Shift+[
Ending double quote "	Ctrl+Shift+]
Bullet ●	Ctrl+Shift+8
En dash –	Ctrl+=
Em dash —	Ctrl+Shift+=
Discretionary hyphen -	Ctrl+- (hyphen)
Nonbreaking hyphen -	Ctrl+Shift+- (hyphen)
Nonbreaking slash /	Ctrl+Shift+/
Nonbreaking backslash \	Ctrl+Shift+\
Section marker §	Ctrl+Shift+6
Paragraph marker ¶	Ctrl+Shift+7
Copyright symbol ©	Ctrl+Shift+C
Registered trademark ®	Ctrl+Shift+R

Text Fields

Use the following key combinations to add fields to text (without accessing the Field dialog box):

Height field	Ctrl+Shift+H or Ctrl+E
Rotation angle field	Ctrl+Shift+A
Width field	Ctrl+Shift+W

Full-screen Navigation

Use these keyboard shortcuts to navigate between Visio and another page when in full-screen view:

Forward	Ctrl+right arrow
Back	Ctrl+left arrow
Next Page	Ctrl+Page Down (not on the numeric keypad)
Previous Page	Ctrl+Page Up (not on the numeric keypad)

Shortcuts by Keystroke

Mouse Buttons

Click	Select shape
Click status line	Size & Position window
Shift + click	Add to or remove from selection set
Double-click	Customized operation
Right-click	Shortcut menu
Ctrl+Shift and click	Zoom in
Ctrl+Shift and drag	Pan
Ctrl+Shift and drag a rectangle	Zoom windowed area
Ctrl+Shift and right-click	Zoom out

Function Keys

F1	Help dialog box
F2	Toggle between text edit and selection mode
F3	Fill dialog box
F4	Repeat last command

F5	Page dialog box
F6	Zoom dialog box
F7	Spelling dialog box
F8	Align Shapes dialog box
F9	Glue toggle (on or off)
F10	Activate menu bar
F11	Text dialog box, Font tab
F12	Save As dialog box
Shift+F3	Line dialog box
Shift+F5	Page Setup dialog box, Print Setup tab
Shift+F6	Zoom out
Shift+F7	Tile windows horizontally
Shift+F9	Snap toggle (on or off)
Shift+F11	Text dialog box, Paragraph tab
Alt+F4	Exit Visio
Alt+F7	Cascade windows
Alt+F8	Macros dialog box
Alt+F9	Snap & Glue dialog box
Alt+F11	Visual Basic Editor
Alt+F12	Save Workspace dialog box
Ctrl+F9	Field dialog box
Ctrl+F11	Text dialog box, Tabs tab
Ctrl+Shift+F7	Tile windows vertically

Ctrl Keys

Ctrl+1	Pointer
Ctrl+2	Text tool
Ctrl+3	Connector tool
Ctrl+4	Pencil tool
Ctrl+5	Freeform tool
Ctrl+6	Line tool

Ctrl+7	Arc tool
Ctrl+8	Rectangle tool
Ctrl+9	Ellipse tool
Ctrl+0 (zero)	Rotation tool
Ctrl+A	Select all
Ctrl+B	Send selected shapes to back
Ctrl+C	Copy to clipboard
Ctrl+D	Duplicate selected shapes
Ctrl+E	Insert height in text field
Ctrl+F	Bring selected shapes to front
Ctrl+G	Group selected shapes
Ctrl+H	Flip horizontal
Ctrl+I	Actual size view (100%)
Ctrl+J	Flip vertical
Ctrl+K	Hyperlinks dialog box
Ctrl+L	Rotate left
Ctrl+M	Carriage return (like pressing the Enter key)
Ctrl+N	New drawing based on current drawing
Ctrl+O	Open dialog box
Ctrl+P	Print dialog box
Ctrl+Q	Exit Visio
Ctrl+R	Rotate right
Ctrl+S	Save drawing
Ctrl+U	Ungroup selected groups
Ctrl+V	Paste from clipboard
Ctrl+W	Whole page view
Ctrl+X	Cut to clipboard
Ctrl+Y	Redo
Ctrl+Z	Undo
Ctrl+Shift+1	Connection point tool
Ctrl+Shift+2	Crop image tool
Ctrl+Shift+3	Stamp tool
Ctrl+Shift+4	Text block tool

Appendix A

Ctrl+Shift+6	Section marker character §
Ctrl+Shift+7	Paragraph marker character ¶
Ctrl+Shift+8	Bullet character ●
Ctrl+Shift+A	Rotation angle text field
Ctrl+Shift+B	**Bold** text format
Ctrl+Shift+C	Copyright symbol character ©
Ctrl+Shift+H	Height text field
Ctrl+Shift+I	*Italic* text format
Ctrl+Shift+R	Registered trademark character ®
Ctrl+Shift+U	Underline text format
Ctrl+Shift+W	Width text field
Ctrl+Shift+X	Sub$_{script}$ text format
Ctrl+Shift+Y	SMALL CAPS text format
Ctrl+Shift+Z	Super^{script} text format
Ctrl+[	Beginning single quote character '
Ctrl+]	Ending single quote character '
Ctrl+=	En dash character –
Ctrl+Shift+/	Nonbreaking slash character /
Ctrl+Shift+\	Nonbreaking backslash character \
Ctrl+Shift+[	Beginning double quote character "
Ctrl+Shift+]	Ending double quote character "
Ctrl+Shift+=	Em dash character —
Ctrl+- (hyphen)	Discretionary hyphen character -
Ctrl+Shift+- (hyphen)	Nonbreaking hyphen character -

Other Keys

Cursor keys (when no objects are selected)	Pan
Select an object, then press cursor keys	Nudge shape
Select object, Shift, and press cursor keys	Pixel nudge
Ctrl+right arrow	Forward (hyperlinking)

Ctrl+left arrow	Back (hyperlinking)
Ctrl+Page Down (not on the numeric keypad)	Next Page (hyperlinking)
Ctrl+Page Up (not on the numeric keypad)	Previous Page (hyperlinking)
Alt	Activate menu bar

Appendix B

Productivity Tips

The following tips help you work more quickly with Visio diagrams.

Opening Additional Stencils

The Geographic Map solution does not open the Flags stencil. To open this stencil (and others), select File | Stencils | Map | Flags from the menu bar. As an alternative, you can click the small down arrow next to the Open Stencil button on the Standard toolbar, then select Map | Flags. Notice that Visio opens the Flags stencil.

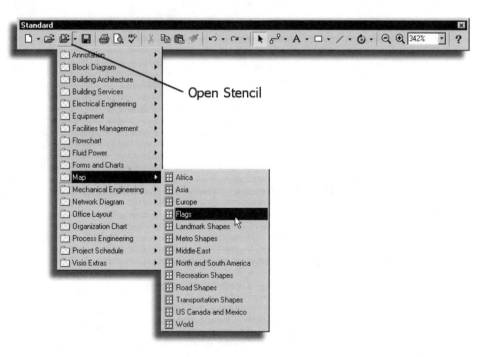

Dragging All Stencil Shapes at Once

Usually, you drag one master at a time from the stencil to the page. When creating a map, you may want to drag <u>all</u> masters onto the page at once. Here's how to do this:

1. Right-click the stencil, and select **Select All**. Notice that all masters are highlighted.

2. Drag any master onto the page; notice that one copy of every master appears as a shape on the page.

Changing the Thickness of Road Shapes

In maps, the thickness of road lines indicates their importance. You can quickly change the thickness of a road line, as follows:

1. Select one or more road lines. To select more than one road shape, hold down the **Ctrl** key while clicking shapes.

2. Right-click, and select **Thick Road, Standard Road**, or **Thin Road**. Notice that the thickness changes.

Connecting All Map Shapes

After dragging geographic map shapes onto the page, you can have Visio "put the map together" correctly and automatically like a jigsaw puzzle, as follows:

1. Press **Ctrl+A** to select all shapes.

2. Right-click any shape, and select **Arrange To Page**. ① (As an alternative, you can select from the menu **Tools | Build Region**—it's the same command, just a different name.) Notice that Visio displays the Arrange To Page dialog box, which asks if you would like Visio to make the completed map fit the page②.

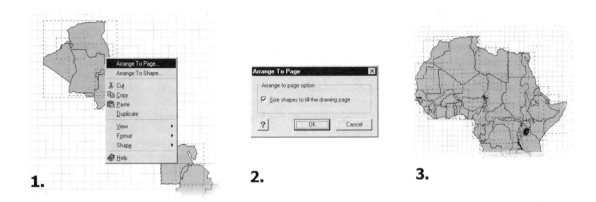

1. 2. 3.

3. Click **OK**. Notice that Visio quickly arranges the shapes into a map③.

Toggling the Display of Layers

The geographic maps place political boundaries on layer Land, rivers on layer Rivers, and lakes on layer Lakes. You can *toggle* (turn off and on) the display of these features by turning on and off the layers:

1. From the menu bar, select **View | Layer Properties.** Notice the Layer Properties dialog box.

2. In the Visible column, click check marks to turn off the display of specific layers ①.

3. In the Print column, click check marks to turn off the printing of specific layers.

4. Click **Apply** to see the effect of your change ②. In the illustration, notice that the lakes and rivers are no longer displayed.

5. Click **OK** to dismiss the dialog box.

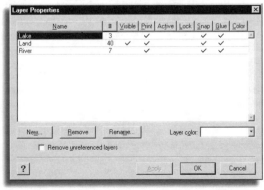

1.

2.

Appendix B

Custom Properties

Each geographic map shape has its name associated as a *custom property* (additional text data). To view the name:

1. Select a map shape.

2. From the menu bar, select **Shape | Custom Properties**. Notice the Custom Properties dialog box.

3. Click **OK** to dismiss the dialog box.

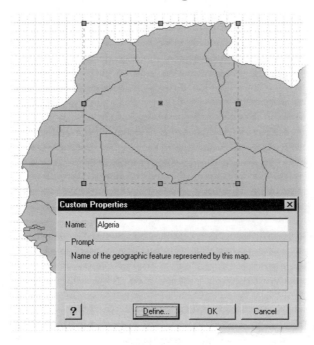

Changing Tree Types

The Tree shape (found in the Landmark Shapes stencil) can change between a deciduous and coniferous tree type. After dragging the shape onto the page, right-click and select the type.

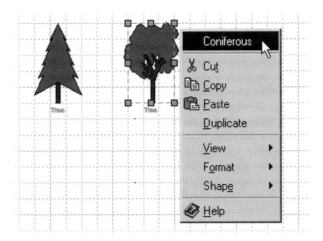

Changing the Calendar's Settings

Once a calendar is in place, you can change all of its settings, such as the starting day of the week (Sunday or Monday). Here's how:

1. Right-click the calendar shape, and select **Properties**. Notice the Custom Properties dialog box.

2. Make changes to the settings.

3. Click **OK**. Notice that the calendar updates automatically to reflect the changes you made.

1.

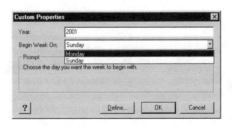

2.

3.

Creating a 12-month Calendar

To create a 12-month calendar with one month on each page:

1. Right-click the page tab ("Page-1" found at the bottom of the drawing area). From the shortcut menu, select **Insert Page**. Notice the Page Setup dialog box.

2. Optionally, change the Name from "Page-2" to the name of a month, such as February. Click **OK**.

3. Repeat for the remaining months of the year. When done, drag the **Large month** master onto each page.

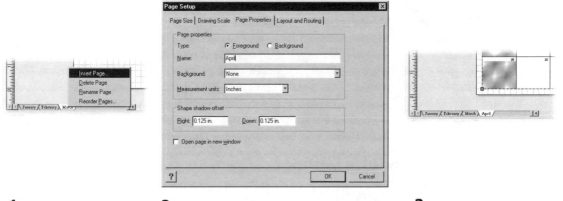

1.   **2.**   **3.**

Dressing up the Calendar

After you create the calendar, you can add shapes. The Calendar Shapes stencil, for example, includes shapes for indicating phases of the moon. You can, in fact, use shapes from any stencil provided with Visio, as well as insert images from other sources, such as photographs, using the Insert | Picture command.

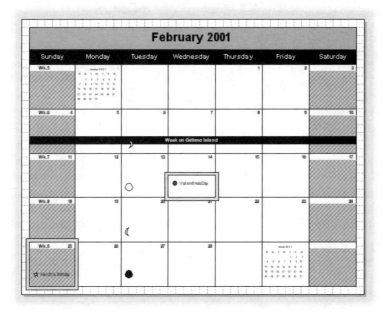

Changing Moon Phases

To change the Moon phases shape, right-click the shape and select one of the phases: First Quarter, Full Moon, Last Quarter, and New Moon.

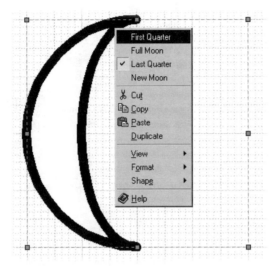

Dressing up the Business Form

After you create the business form, you can use shapes from any stencil, including backgrounds from the Background Shapes stencil. In addition, you can insert images from other sources, such as clip art and photographs, using the Insert | Picture command.

Making Copies of Business Cards

A page can fit about ten business cards. After designing one card, make nine identical copies as follows:

1.   Copy one card: Hold down the **Ctrl** key and drag the card horizontally. Notice that Visio makes a copy.

2.   Copy two cards: hold down the **Shift** key to select both cards. Hold down the **Ctrl** key and drag the cards vertically. Notice that Visio makes two copies.

3.   Press function key **F4** until you have a total of ten business cards.

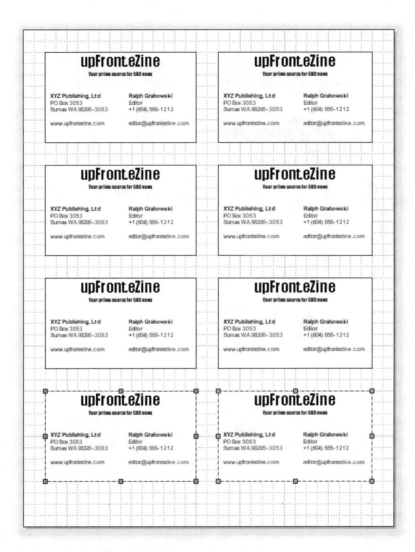

Save It 2000

Save It 2000 is an add-on that automatically saves all drawings open in Visio 2000 based on a user-defined interval. You can download this utility from http://www.visio.com/files/downloads/save it 2000.exe.

Acronyms

Microsoft has a list of acronyms at: http://www.microsoft.com/HWDEV/acronym.htm.

Subscribe to Visions.eZine

Visions.eZine is the newsletter for Visio and IntelliCAD users. Every two weeks, the newsletter is delivered by e-mail for free. The newsletter includes news of Visio, IntelliCAD, Microsoft, and the computer world. It includes tips, interesting Web sites to visit, and a listing of the latest books about Visio. To subscribe, send the message "subscribe visions" to ralphg@xyzpress.com.

Appendix C

Quiz Answers

Lesson 1

1. True
2. (a) Ctrl   (ii)   Hold down the Ctrl key.
   (b) Shift   (iv)   Hold down the Shift key.
   (c) Ctrl+N   (v)   Start a new drawing.
   (d) Ctrl+Z   (iii) Undo.
   (e) Ctrl+Y   (i)   Redo.
3. False; Visio can open drawings created by other software packages.
4. (c) Master.
5. False; a Visio drawing can contain many pages.
6. (a) Can be any size.
7. False; gridlines are not printed.
8. (d) Explains the purpose of a toolbar button.
9. (b) Resizing the shape.
10. (c) The cursor is not over a shape.

Lesson 2

1. (b) Create maps showing country borders.
2. (a) Create maps showing visitors how to get to your house.
3. (d) Build Region.
4. (a) Master.
5. True
6. (a) Ctrl+A   (iii) Select All.
   (b) Ctrl+B   (ii)   Move to back.

(c)   Ctrl+P   (v)   Print drawing.

(d)   Ctrl+S   (i)   Save file.

(e)   Ctrl+N   (iv)   Start a new drawing.

7. (b)   Click the Rotation tool, then drag a handle around.

8. (c)   Shape.

9. (d)   Shift key.

10. False

Lesson 3

1. (c)   Create a month planner.

2. (a)   Right-click the shape and select the phase.

3. (d)   Cannot be changed in size.

4. (c)   Drag a handle outward from the shape.

5. (c)   Text tool.

6. (d)   Drag an end handle inward toward the shape's center.

7. (c)   Both of the above.

8. (d)   None of the above.

9. True

10. False

Lesson 4

1. (b)   Ctrl

2. (c)   Repeat the last command.

3. (a)   Small red square   (iii)   Shape is attached to another shape.

    (b)   Green square   (iv)   Shape can be stretched.

    (c)   Cyan square   (i)   Second selected shape.

    (d)   Gray padlock   (v)   Shape cannot be stretched.

    (e)   Large red square   (ii)   Shape is glued to another shape.

4. True

5. (d)   Aligning objects.

6. (a)   Select the shapes and press Ctrl+G.

7. False

8. True

9. (c)   Making text bold.

10. True

Lesson 5

1. True
2. False
3. (c)   1/72 inch.
4. (a)   Ctrl+A   (iii)   Select All.
    (b)   Ctrl+1   (i)   Pointer tool.
    (c)   Ctrl+drag   (v)   Copy shapes.
    (d)   Ctrl+K   (ii)   Insert or Edit Hyperlinks.
    (e)   Ctrl+Tab   (iv)   Switch to another drawing in Visio.
5. (d)   All of the above.
6. (b)   To link to another file or an Internet location.
7. True
8. (a)   Change the color of all shapes at once.
9. (c)   Double-click the shape.
10. True

Lesson 6

1. (b)   Drop one shape on the other.
2. (c)   A shape above another shape in the reporting structure.
3. (a)   A shape below another shape in the reporting structure.
4. True
5. (a)   Creating a second page in the org chart diagram.
6. (b)   Changing an org shape from one type to another.
7. (d)   There is no such command in Visio 2000.
8. (d)   Excel and ASCII.
9. False
10. True

Lesson 7

1. (c)   Keeps track of the phases of a project.
2. (b)   Bytes
3. True
4. False
5. (a)   ID

6. (a) m   (iii)   minute
    (b) d   (i)   day
    (c) h   (iv)   hour
    (d) w   (ii)   week

7. (a) CSV   (iii)   Comma-delimited text
    (b) MPX   (i)   Microsoft Project Exchange
    (c) TXT   (iv)   Tab-delimited text
    (d) XLS   (ii)   Microsoft Excel

8. (c) Both of the above.

9. True

10. False

Lesson 8

1. False; network diagrams must be created manually.

2. True

3. True

4. (b) The connector is glued to the shape.

5. (c) Moving the shape drags the connector with it.

6. (d) Ctrl+Z

7. False; the Layer Properties dialog box displays the number of shapes on each layer.

8. True

9. False; all shapes can have custom properties.

10. True

Lesson 9

1. (b) Make the drawing fit the page.

2. (a) 12"

3. (c) ¼"

4. True

5. (c) All of the above.

6. (a) Ctrl+B   (iii)   Move object to the background.
    (b) Ctrl+F   (iv)   Move object to the foreground.
    (c) Ctrl+Shift+B   (ii)   Make text bold.
    (d) Ctrl+K   (i)   Insert hyperlink.

7. (d)   96"

8. False; the zero point can be repositioned with Ctrl+drag.

9. (b)   Details can be lost.

10. (a)   The ability to zoom and pan the image without loss of resolution.

Answer to exercise #1:

33' x 21'

Lesson 10

1. (c)   Simulates 3-D in a 2-D environment.

2. (a)   2-D   (ii)   Two dimensional
   (b)   3-D   (iv)   Three dimensional
   (c)   DWG   (iii)   Drawing file
   (d)   DXF   (v)   Drawing interchange file
   (e)   CAD   (i)   Computer-aided design

3. True

4. False; color changes only when the colors are assigned by layer in the CAD drawing.

5. (a)   Width of lines.

6. False; the CAD drawing can be modified.

7. (b)   Use the Rotation tool.

8. (c)   Ellipse.

9. (b)   Draw an ellipse and rotate it to –60 degrees.

10. False; Visio cannot oblique text to make it look correct in an isometric drawing.

Index

Other Visio Titles from Wordware

Learn Visio 2000

For users of Visio 2000 Standard Edition, Technical Edition, Professional Edition, and Enterprise Edition

Ralph Grabowski

Visio is essential office software for creating structured business diagrams, such as flowcharts, site maps, and organization charts. To support the more than three million users of this software, best-selling Visio author Ralph Grabowski provides comprehensive coverage of Visio 2000. His modular format allows the user to start anywhere in the book to solve a particular problem. Among the new features of Visio 2000 is the Drawing Explorer, which presents drawing content in an Explorer-like tree structure that enables the user to see the layers, pages, and shapes that make up a drawing. Those interested in creating web pages can now save drawings in VML format, in addition to HTML, for viewing by web browsers. In addition, Visio 2000 presents changes to the user interface and fully customizable toolbars.

424 pp. • 7½ x 9¼
1-55622-673-X • $29.95

Level: Introductory to intermediate
Category: Visio 2000/business graphics

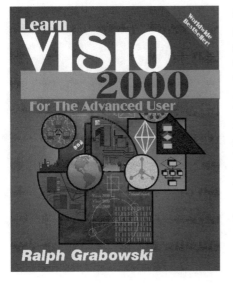

Learn Visio 2000 for the Advanced User

For users of Visio 2000 Standard Edition, Technical Edition, Professional Edition, and Enterprise Edition

Ralph Grabowski

With more than three million users worldwide, Visio is one of the most successful business graphics software packages on the market. Visio's intuitive drag-and-drop approach allows beginners to create drawings such as diagrams, charts, and schematics. For advanced users, Visio contains powerful tools for enhanced productivity. This title from Ralph Grabowski primarily emphasizes the customization features found in Visio, which enable the user to adapt the software to particular functions. Among these features are masters and styles, stencils and templates, and the ShapeSheet. Step-by-step tutorials guide you through these customization techniques. The companion CD-ROM contains example files to support the hands-on activities in the book.

376 pp. • 7½ x 9¼ • Includes CD
1-55622-711-6 • $34.95

Level: Intermediate to advanced
Category: Visio 2000/business graphics

I don't have time for learning curves.

[1]Expert

technical [2]
reference

[3]code

[4] now

[5] EarthWeb's
ITKnowledge℠

They rely on you to be the ❶ expert on tough development challenges. There's no time for learning curves, so you go online for ❷ technical references from the experts who wrote the books. Find answers fast simply by clicking on our search engine. Access hundreds of online books, tutorials and even source ❸ code samples ❹ now. Go to ❺ EarthWeb's ITKnowledge, get immediate answers, and get down to it.

Get your FREE ITKnowledge trial subscription today at itkgo.com.
Use code number 026.

EARTHWEB
Go further *faster*

About the CD

The companion CD-ROM contains the files used in the basic and advanced tutorials, along with diagrams that show the result of the tutorials.

Simply use Windows Explorer to copy the files to your hard drive.

WARNING: Opening the CD package makes this book non-returnable.

CD/Source Code Usage License Agreement

Please read the following CD/Source Code usage license agreement before opening the CD and using the contents therein:

1. By opening the accompanying software package, you are indicating that you have read and agree to be bound by all terms and conditions of this CD/Source Code usage license agreement.
2. The compilation of code and utilities contained on the CD and in the book are copyrighted and protected by both U.S. copyright law and international copyright treaties, and is owned by Wordware Publishing, Inc. Individual source code, example programs, help files, freeware, shareware, utilities, and evaluation packages, including their copyrights, are owned by the respective authors.
3. No part of the enclosed CD or this book, including all source code, help files, shareware, freeware, utilities, example programs, or evaluation programs, may be made available on a public forum (such as a World Wide Web page, FTP site, bulletin board, or Internet news group) without the express written permission of Wordware Publishing, Inc. or the author of the respective source code, help files, shareware, freeware, utilities, example programs, or evaluation programs.
4. You may not decompile, reverse engineer, disassemble, create a derivative work, or otherwise use the enclosed programs, help files, freeware, shareware, utilities, or evaluation programs except as stated in this agreement.
5. The software, contained on the CD and/or as source code in this book, is sold without warranty of any kind. Wordware Publishing, Inc. and the authors specifically disclaim all other warranties, express or implied, including but not limited to implied warranties of merchantability and fitness for a particular purpose with respect to defects in the disk, the program, source code, sample files, help files, freeware, shareware, utilities, and evaluation programs contained therein, and/or the techniques described in the book and implemented in the example programs. In no event shall Wordware Publishing, Inc., its dealers, its distributors, or the authors be liable or held responsible for any loss of profit or any other alleged or actual private or commercial damage, including but not limited to special, incidental, consequential, or other damages.
6. One (1) copy of the CD or any source code therein may be created for backup purposes. The CD and all accompanying source code, sample files, help files, freeware, shareware, utilities, and evaluation programs may be copied to your hard drive. With the exception of freeware and shareware programs, at no time can any part of the contents of this CD reside on more than one computer at one time. The contents of the CD can be copied to another computer, as long as the contents of the CD contained on the original computer are deleted.
7. You may not include any part of the CD contents, including all source code, example programs, shareware, freeware, help files, utilities, or evaluation programs in any compilation of source code, utilities, help files, example programs, freeware, shareware, or evaluation programs on any media, including but not limited to CD, disk, or Internet distribution, without the express written permission of Wordware Publishing, Inc. or the owner of the individual source code, utilities, help files, example programs, freeware, shareware, or evaluation programs.
8. You may use the source code, techniques, and example programs in your own commercial or private applications unless otherwise noted by additional usage agreements as found on the CD.